✝ A ✝ ✝ O O

ALPHABETS AND SCRIPTS

VINCE HEMINGSON

✝ A ✝ ✝ O O

ALPHABETS AND SCRIPTS

AN ESSENTIAL REFERENCE FOR BODY ART

VINCE HEMINGSON

A & C BLACK

First published in 2009 by
A&C Black Publishers
36 Soho Square
London W1D 3QY
www.acblack.com

ISBN: 978-1-4081-2838-1

Copyright © Quintet Publishing Limited 2009

This book was conceived, designed and produced by
Quintet Publishing Limited
6 Blundell Street
London N7 9BH
UK

QTT.ASTD

Project Editors: Martha Burley, Asha Savjani
Art Director: Michael Charles
Designer: MD Design
Illustrators: Bernard Chau, David Schmeikal
Managing Editor: Donna Gregory
Publisher: James Tavendale

CIP Catalogue records for this book are available from the British Library and the
US Library of Congress.

Printed in China by Midas Printing International Limited

10 9 8 7 6 5 4 3 2 1

TATTOO
ALPHABETS AND SCRIPTS
CONTENTS

FOREWORD

Vince Hemingson has authored a new book, this time on tattoo typography. Although I am no authority on the etymology of typefaces, written symbols and characters, alphabets and such, Vince contacted me about writing a foreword for his manuscript, much as I had done for his excellent *Tattoo Design Directory*, which was published a year ago. My fears of getting in over my head were quickly allayed, when I noticed on the first page a reference to the phrase 'I Love Mary' as being the kind of text tattoo that the book was going to talk about. The fact is, I have a tattoo, LITTLE MARY, tattooed on my shinbone in honor of my beautiful wife, and, although it doesn't exactly say 'I Love Mary' it's pretty damn close. In any case, enough to kindle my interest.

This book was perfect for me. I was especially intrigued when several industry experts like C.W. Eldridge, 'Shanghai' Kate Hellenbrand and Thomas Lockhart, along with Daniel Will-Harris and Ina Saltz (a couple of renowned academics) described,

philosophised and informally chatted about the art and study of lettering, text and the veritable plethora of calligraphic symbols. Very cool stuff. In fact, I learned quite a bit and I was only on page 21.

A test of a book about typefaces, alphabets, their history and use as tattoo art is whether or not the best letterer I have ever seen, Jack Rudy, is mentioned. Well, Jack is mentioned, as are other lettering legends Good Time Charlie Cartwright and Freddy Negrete, along with cinema diva Angelina Jolie, who is on a page captioned 'Viking Runes', which just goes to show how far and diverse Vince's research has taken him. Latin, Sanskrit, Hebrew, Cyrillic, Japanese kanji, Roman, hieroglyphics, you name it, not only does Vince describe their origins and development, but showcases page after page of words that are not only meaningful but absolutely ideal for tattoo work. And just when you think the book can't possibly maintain this pace, along comes over fifty pages of fonts, logos and

Thai Buddhists are known to cover large parts of the body with sacred tattoos – seen to protect

all manner of written letters and scribbles, all presented side by side with sample sentences, so you can see exactly how these alphabets look when gathered together into familiar words and various heartfelt phrases.

I really like Vince's book. It's informative, beautifully laid out and useful, especially if you are a practitioner or serious aficionado of tattoo art. I'm certain that even longtime sign-painters-turned-tattooists like Henry Goldfield, Dave Shore and Uncle Tim Heitkotter will enjoy flipping through the pages. Yes, this is a book for the experienced, but it is also for neophytes who are planning a first tattoo. Once again, a perfect example of the unpredictability and intriguing variety in the colourful world of tattoo.

Bob Baxter, Editor-in-Chief
Skin&Ink Magazine

introduction

Text tattoos and tattoo typography make up a genre of body art that is particularly focused on the message. A single word, or a line of poetry or prose, a passage from a religious text, a lyric from a song, all have the power to convey concise meaning with enormous emotional impact.

Whether subtle or overt, all tattoos symbolise something to the wearer, whether simply a butterfly representing feminine beauty, or the more profound significance of the image of Christ crucified on the Cross. Context is everything when it comes to symbolism. Depending upon your cultural reference point, a wolf may symbolise swiftness and cunning, courage and loyalty, a spirit guide, a creator figure or a shape-shifter. What matters is what a wolf means to you.

Of course, words can also have more than one meaning. You need only open a dictionary to see that this is so. However, text tattoos usually spell out their symbolism for us. They are often specific declarations of intent and belief.

The immense popularity of Japanese kanji tattoos or Chinese character tattoos in the West can, in large part, be attributed to the mysterious nature of a text symbol with which most of us are unfamiliar. The same attraction is implicit in text tattoos using the Persian, Hebrew, Greek or Latin languages, or Egyptian hieroglyphs. English-language tattoos are some of the most popular body art designs among the young in China today.

the message

Text tattoos are often used as declarations of love and friendship, are integral to memorial and patriotic tattoos for the specific information they can convey and often signify inclusion or membership of a tribe or group. But be forewarned, there is no category of tattoos that carries greater potential for regret than text tattoos – especially when the tattoo contains the name or initials of a former lover or significant other. Yet tattoos of hearts and flowers with tender declarations of everlasting love continue to pay the rent for tattoo artists. First when the tattoo 'I love Mary' is inked in a scroll beneath a red rose, and again when the name is covered up with some artfully inked leaves. Still, it must be said that there are many pledges of love that people do not regret. The heart tattoo inscribed with 'I love Mum' was popularised by soldiers going to war, and reminded homesick soldiers or sailors of why they were there and for whom they were fighting, as well as serving as poignant reminders of the life left behind.

Memorial tattoos, that commemorate a lost love, a child, a family member or a friend who has passed away suddenly and unexpectedly, use text to spell out the loss. Such tattoos are popular among members of the armed services, policemen and firefighters who wish to memorialise a fallen comrade, and in a way they allow people to grieve for a loved one, and honour their memory as they try to get on with their own lives.

TATTOO TYPOGRAPHY

As a writer, I pride myself on having at least a working grasp of the significance of language and the importance of specific words or phrases as they relate to text tattoos. But in the weeks and months researching typography and the art and graphic design inherent in the creation and evolution of typefaces and fonts, I was nearly overcome by the sheer volume of information.

Typography, or as my researcher, PJ Reece, and I came to think of it, 'tattoo typography', is a huge field of artistic endeavour, and an art form in itself. The language of typography is itself wonderful, filled as it is with descriptions of typefaces and fonts – cursive, serif and sans-serif; flourishes and strokes; ligatures; kerning; tracking; sizing; and spacing – until the mind positively reels. You can spend a lifetime working in typography, and many choose to do so.

THOUGHTS FROM THE PROFESSIONALS

Blackletter fonts work well for simple, large text tattoos with high impact

THE TYPOGRAPHERS

Ina Saltz (*IS*) and Daniel Will-Harris (*DWH*) are two leading authorities on typography and design who have offered their unique insight into typography as it relates to tattoos and body art.

Ina Saltz is an art director and professor at The City College of New York, whose areas of expertise include typography and magazine design. She is author of the hugely popular and widely acclaimed book, *Body Type: Intimate Messages Etched in the Flesh*.

Daniel Will-Harris is a prolific writer and designer, described by the New York Museum of Modern Art as a 'computer graphics pioneer' whose work is 'truly unique'. As a typography expert, Will-Harris created the website, Esperfonto.

Q: As a typographer and designer, what advice would you give to a tattoo artist looking to create a text tattoo that both meets the needs of their client, and is in and of itself a good design?
IS: I would counsel that the typeface chosen for the tattoo should enhance, amplify and support the content of the message. The emotional tone of the style should

match the tone of the message. For example, a literary quote might be expressed in a classic book font like Garamond or Caslon. Something poetic might look best in a script, for example, Bickham Script. There are many books and online tutorials available on good typographic usage. You can never know too much about type! But be wary of novelty typefaces, which go out of style as quickly as they came in. Stick with the classics for good design longevity.

DWH: Tattoos are a form of communication. Any time you have a word, or even a letter, you also have the choice of type style or typeface – and your choice becomes an integral part of that communication and how it feels. You have to decide what typeface will help your design.

Too many artists just go to 'stock Goth' (a style of type also known as Blackletter). These are traditional – and overused. If a Gothic letter is what someone asks for specifically, that's OK – if it really has some meaning for the client. But as an artist, you can give them more than what is expected.

Depending on what the customer wants their tattoo to feel like, and depending on your artistic style, chances are there are many typefaces that will have more feeling and impact than 'stock Goth'.

I believe there's only one rule of typography: be appropriate. Type is both about style and emotion – what kind of impression you want to convey. Going only for style can work – but it can also be superficial. So get to know a lot of fonts – that way you have a choice, and instead of going back to the same one or two you always use, you have the knowledge to find one that really kicks your design to the next level – one that has an emotional connection as well as being even more unique.

> '...AS AN ARTIST, YOU CAN GIVE SOMEONE MORE THAN WHAT IS EXPECTED'
>
> DANIEL WILL-HARRIS

There's no right answer, no one universal typeface that's good for every design. So if you're giving people the same font over and over again, then you could be doing a lot better.

Leading typographer Daniel Will-Harris

So – what's a good font? I recommend finding a typeface personality. Remember, another name for individual letters in a font is 'characters', so you want to find 'characters with character'. By that I mean that when you look at the typeface, it speaks to you. One that makes you think, 'that's fun or dark or fractured or elegant, artistic, bold, sweet, retro...'. And more than that, one that makes you feel something – warm, cool, friendly, serious, fun, frightening – however you want it to feel.

Generally, generic faces, such as Times Roman or Arial, Helvetica and Verdana, are bland. Yet there might be times you want to use them for just that reason – but do choose them for a reason, not just because they're handy and easy to print out as they're already on your computer!

Q: How would you define a good text tattoo?
IS: A good text tattoo is sharp, crisp and highly detailed; it accurately replicates the typeface (if it is a typeface); it is typographically well drawn; if it is custom hand lettering, it follows the line of the body part; and above all, is an appropriate style for the content of the text. Lettering artistry is a specialised field, and there are those who have a feeling for letterforms and understand how to balance legibility and beauty in a disciplined way that is true to the long history of alphabetic design. Try to find a tattoo artist who has an affinity for and sensitivity to letterforms.

Q: What strikes you as a remarkable text tattoo, one that truly stands out from the rest?
IS: I have seen many spectacular text tattoos, both lengthy passages of text and single characters. One

particularly gorgeous passage of text was from Dante's *Inferno*, in tight rows of circles of classic roman capitals around the subject's upper arm. A single letter 'S' on a woman's lower back was a deliriously and elaborately flourished example from a sixteenth-century German book on calligraphy.

DWH: For me, personally, I love handwritten script tattoos. Calligraphy is an art almost as ancient as tattooing, and like tattoos, it's a form of communication. So when a tattoo artist is also a calligrapher that shows even more skill.

I love calligraphic tattoos that become necklaces or armbands.

That said, I also like any text tattoo where the typeface has been chosen to reflect the content. If the illustration is Japanese, then it's lovely to use a typeface such as ITC Arid, or Flood. If a design is classical, and you want something that looks Greco-Roman, there are faces such as Trajan or Sophia that will give you the right flavour and feeling.

> 'A GOOD TEXT TATTOO IS SHARP, CRISP AND HIGHLY DETAILED...'
>
> INA SALTZ

Q: Do you see common or recurring mistakes in text tattoos?
IS: I often see blurry edges, lettering that is not aligned on the baseline, poor kerning [letter spacing] or word spacing, too much or too little leading [line spacing]. Or sometimes badly rendered letterforms. Sometimes the placement of the tattoo is wrong; it does not sit well on the body part. Type is specialised and different from images, which do not rely on a baseline and a linear flow. A good tattoo artist will take these factors into consideration.

Q: For someone considering the choice of a text tattoo, what advice would you give?
IS: In terms of form, the size of the text is important; it should not be so small that the counter spaces [the spaces inside the letters] and the spaces between the letters will close up over time as the tattoo ages. The choice of type style is critical,

too; typefaces with a larger x-height [x-height refers to the height of a lower-case x as compared to the ascenders and descenders, which are the parts of the letters that extend above and below the x-height, for example, the tail of the 'g' or the top of a 'b'] will hold up better than those with a small x-height.

DWH: Do your own research! Go to my site, Esperfonto, choose various feelings and impressions, and see what it suggests. Browse font sites like My Fonts and see if a font speaks to you – once you've started to look at more and more fonts, you'll appreciate how different they can be, and how much feeling they can convey, and you won't settle for 'stock Goth' just because it's handy.

You can also set the words of your tattoo in various fonts and see what it will look like. Some words just look better in different typefaces. You might find a typeface you love, but the words you want to set don't look as good in it.

Q: Do you have a favourite tattoo typeface? A list of typefaces you consider best for body art?
IS: Again, it depends on the

message. I have several favourites in different categories; for a sans-serif, Helvetica is a good neutral face with a wide range of weights and widths. I also love the sans-serif typeface Verdana, designed by Matthew Carter. In the serif category, I love Georgia, also designed by Matthew Carter, because it is classic but a bit weightier than some of its serif compatriots. But there are many beautiful typefaces that will work well for tattoos; Zapfino is beautiful for a single word or just a few words, with its flamboyantly extended flourishes.

DWH: It's all about personal preference – or, if you're going for a particular time period, say seventeenth-century pirate, knowing what typeface or style will be accurate or at least look realistic.

If I were getting a tattoo that wasn't calligraphic, I'd probably use GM Nanogram – simply because I love the fun simplicity of it, or perhaps Flood, because I like the Japanese brushstroke look

> 'THE CHOICE OF TYPESTYLE IS CRITICAL...'
> INA SALTZ

of it. Or something Art Deco like DecoGlass for a subtle armband.

Q: Is there one text tattoo that stands out in your memory as being truly memorable?

IS: This is like asking a mother which of her children is her favourite! There is one that is a very large, black question mark, where the nipple is the dot under the question mark. That's pretty memorable, from a visual standpoint. But it is hard for me to separate the tattoos from the stories behind them, so some of the most memorable ones for me are the ones that have the most unusual back-stories. I have met some of the most remarkable and unusual people through my documentation of typographic tattoos; their stories and their lives have enriched my perspectives and my outlook on humanity. That is why I hope to continue researching this area for many years to come.

Author and professor Ina Saltz

typefaces themselves. He also had some Pantone colour swatch tattoos.

The most moving ones, though, are always the most personal, the name of a loved one, a line of poetry or lyrics from a special song.

Q: In your opinion, what is it about a text tattoo that sets them apart from other genres and forms of body art?

IS: Text sends a specific, very literal message, though it may have a subliminal subtext. People who have typographic tattoos tend to have a precise message they wish to convey. Images can be variously interpreted.

DWH: Jeffrey Sebelia's, because it was the first of its kind I'd seen and because the calligraphy is beautiful. And I met a designer who had a list of his favourite typefaces tattooed on his arm – in the

DWH: Words add an extra level of meaning, they literally send a message.

Q: How important do you think it is for a tattoo artist to have working knowledge about ligatures, kerning and tracking when designing text tattoos?

IS: Many tattoo artists today (especially the younger ones) have a background in graphic design and may have actually studied typography in art school. So they might be better equipped to design and execute a typographic tattoo. However, typography is a very complex area of design and even many professional designers have only a rudimentary knowledge of type. The more the artist knows about type usage, the better. Also, some tattoo artists take special pride in their lettering, especially their custom lettering work. Those are the ones to look for. Oddly, many tattoo artists do not consider text their best work; it doesn't seem as creative to them, and they often look upon it as just another paying assignment. On the contrary, typographic tattoos require more skill than image-based tattoos,

> 'A SINGLE LETTER CAN BE AS INTERESTING AND EXOTIC AS AN ILLU-STRATION'
> Daniel Will-Harris

because there is much less margin for error.

DWH: Of all those, the only important one is kerning – which is basically the artistic spacing of letters so that they look even or right. Shifting an individual letter a little to the left or right can make it look more even – and also make it easier to read. Sometimes there's too much space between two letters, often the first, which is a capital, and then it almost makes the word read like two words, which, depending on the words, could be unfortunate!

I often see tattoos where the letters are all spaced out – to fit around a neck. Again, you have to do this carefully so it's still readable as a word or words and doesn't end up looking like a bunch of separate letters.

Q: What advice would you give about sizing and spacing of text tattoos in relation to the human body?

IS: The larger the tattoo, the more legible and distinct it will be. At small sizes, text tattoos can fill in [the lines might bleed slightly and obliterate the spaces inside the letters, or between the letters] so, depending on the style chosen to best represent the content of the text, the artist may need to make tiny adjustments by opening up the letter spacing.

'YOU HAVE THE ENTIRE WORLD OF TYPE AT YOUR FINGERTIPS'
DANIEL WILL-HARRIS

DWH: I don't think there's one right answer to that. If someone wanted a giant letter 'A' tattooed on their chest – just one letter, that could be cool. Or a giant 'Z' like Zorro. That's fine. On the small size, you just want to make sure it's big enough to read.

I think people can do more with letterforms, the shape of each letter, as graphics themselves. A single letter, in a distinctive typeface, can be as interesting and exotic as an illustration. When you start to look at the shapes of letters, especially what are called display faces (used for headlines), or script faces, you see such beautiful evocative shapes – and they're letters, too. So if you want to monogram yourself, it doesn't just have to be block letters or cheesy old scripts like you see on shirt monograms. You have the entire world of type at your fingertips now – so spend some time looking at fonts, and you will see there's a whole world of unique shapes that do more than just spell things – they bring ideas, memories and feelings to mind.

Seize the day
Carpe Diem
Adobe Caslon Regular

To love and to cherish
Ut Amem Et Foveam
Bickham Script Regular

the tattoo artists

After gleaning such useful insights from Saltz and Will-Harris about typography and its application to text tattoos, I sought out the wisdom of a number of tattoo artists, some with three and four decades of experience.

Thomas Lockhart

Thomas Lockhart has been tattooing for more than three decades, and his shop, West Coast Tattoo, is the oldest continually operated tattoo shop in Canada. He offers his clients hundreds of books of reference material to search through. Lockhart's advice was concise and to the point.

'There are thousands of fonts that will work', says Lockhart, 'depending on the tattoo design and what the customer wants. The single biggest piece of advice you can give people is don't go too small. You do not want a tattoo where the ink will bleed and obliterate the open spaces in the lettering and create a "black

> '...DON'T GO TOO SMALL. THE INK WILL BLEED AND OBLITERATE THE OPEN SPACES IN THE LETTERING'
> Thomas Lockhart

blob" with the passage of time. Other than that, you need to remind people that there are no straight lines in the human body. We're made up of curves and good tattoos follow the natural lines and contours of the human form in a way that is aesthetically pleasing to the eye.'

Echoing the viewpoint of Chuck Eldridge, Lockhart added, 'Printing inside banners and ribbons is one thing, and any reasonably talented tattoo artist can pull that off. But large lettering, where the text is the tattoo design, is much harder than it looks. I think it's a speciality. Doing great lettering is no different than doing great Japanese. If your heart is set on getting a great text tattoo you should find the right artist for the job. Guys like Jack Rudy and a whole new generation of artists in Southern California are doing amazing work with script, graffiti and lettering because it's so much a part of that Californian culture.'

SHANGHAI KATE

Kate 'Shanghai Kate' Hellenbrand has, over the course of her career, worked with, among many others, such tattoo luminaries as Mike Malone, Ed Hardy and Sailor Jerry. She started out as graphic designer with a deep love for typography. 'The most important thing to remember about type on the body is correct size and readability. Too many people copy script directly from a book and slap it on. Well, it won't last and it will blur. Kerning is important as well as maintaining the proper size of upper to lower case. Never do type in script in all caps!' Hellebrand continues, 'Old English and derivations of it are really good as long as you watch the "I", "J", "T", "U", and "V" and can make adjustments to those to make them more readable.'

THE TATTOOED DESIGNERS

Dave Schmeikal, Chris Hold and Shannon Hemmett are a group of graphic designers and artists in their late twenties and early thirties. They share a love and passion for body art, so much so that they each could be accurately described as being 'heavily' tattooed. Chris is so devoted to body art that he has spent the past three years dividing his time between the design studio and the tattoo studio. The following is from a round-robin discussion, a distillation of the answers to questions similar to those I put to Ina Saltz and Daniel Will-Harris.

CHRIS HOLD

'At the risk of sounding like a purist, the body is not a sheet of paper, it is not a page in a book, nor is it a flat computer screen. Compare hand-lettered samples from Sailor Jerry, Boog, El Chino, Jack Rudy and Rezine. In my opinion, there's no comparison for quality between the hand-drawn lettering and the font produced – say Franklin Gothic for example – out of a computer printer. You can't slap a two-dimensional design on the human body like a decal.

'The body is organic, curved, asymmetrical and covered with irregularities: moles, pores, birthmarks, scars, etc. It's not reasonable (or fair) to expect flesh to live up to the crispness, clarity and geometric perfection possible with a 600 dpi printer. Time is not kind to the edges and corners of most typeface tattoos. I think they tend to fade and age badly. Ink-spread is inevitable in a tattoo design on the body and not accounting for it in one's lettering results in closed-in counters, blobby serifs and ultimately, unreadable tattoos.

'What's the solution? Pick up old calligraphy books and learn foundational lettering structure. Use a dip nib pen and brush. Inevitably when lettering something by hand, many opportunities for nuance and flourishes become apparent. If you ignore the basics of lettering you're blind to the reasonable, natural variations that can be introduced into a word or phrase to make it flow and fit the form it's intended for.

'I think typefaces are most useful as a jumping-off point – in the hands of someone that understands and cares about lettering. Tattoo artists need to convey that to their customers and fully explain the limitations inherent in tattoo designs and in the skin as a canvas. Tattoo design works best when they collaborate with the artist.'

SHANNON HEMMETT
'I echo Chris' thoughts in many aspects, so I'll try not to repeat what has already been shared. I am not a fan of font tattoos either. Multi-dimensional skin is not an ideal canvas for the obsessive mathematical elements inherent in print-based typography.

'I've found that typewriter faces sometimes translate well as text tattoo designs, depending on the context and placement. Typewriter styled letters are tactile, usually a little imperfect and become even more flawed with age (on skin and paper), which probably explains why I feel they are more "tattoo-able" than ultra-rigid examples like Franklin Gothic or Helvetica.

'Basic typography rules still apply when creating or commissioning your own lettering. Kerning is important for flow, rhythm and readability. I agree with Kate Hellenbrand that you should never use all uppercase letters for script. You would never typeset a printed wedding invitation in all caps, and the same rule applies for skin. It's simply unreadable. Do not stack letters vertically unless your language of choice calls for it. It's illegible and irritating to have to spell something out vertically before you inevitably reorient the tattoo horizontally in your mind's eye.

'When I decided to get my script tattoo (Shannon has a large chest piece), the artist and I mulled over the quote for a good while and considered how it was perceived, read and heard aloud before proceeding with the tattoo. I encourage everyone to take the time to go through this process. Read it aloud to others, say it to yourself and get others to read it to you. Really listen to the words and think about the rhythm they create.'

Dave Schmeikal

Dave Schmeikal added, 'I am definitely in agreement with Chris and Shannon in regards to the "right" font to put on skin. For me, the most successful text tattoos are ones that choose a font that I would describe as "organic".

'For this reason, I am really drawn to well-executed "graffiti" tattoo designs. At first glance the design may not be instantly legible, but like most graffiti a little more analysis provides you with the message hidden in its linework. I want

someone to have to work a little to try and decipher the message in my work. You don't always want to be obvious.

'I think Chris was really on to something when he suggested that text tattoo designs need to be created or rendered by hand for the design to have a chance to be successful on skin. Great tattoo designs take advantage of the negative space within the design and the artist understands that the rules that apply to typesetting in two-dimensional formats don't readily transfer to three-dimensional forms like the human body. There is of course an exception for every rule.

'Trying to keep a typeset consistency that is required on paper oftentimes doesn't translate well when working on skin. Frankly, I don't think that large quantities of identical text make for a great tattoo. I prefer hybrids of "custom" letters and graffiti.

'In the end, the literal message that a text tattoo provides can be moving, powerful, even humorous and can really capture the desired mood better than an image all on its own.'

The whys and hows of words

A picture may paint a thousand words, but there are times in life when a few well-chosen words can speak volumes and move mountains.

A heart tattoo is one thing, but one that says 'Mum' or 'Dad' in a ribbon or scroll across the heart is taken to an entirely different level of meaning and emotional impact. Getting a tattoo with the name or the initials of the one you love can be a greater commitment than getting married. You may part ways with the one you once loved, but the tattoo will most assuredly still be there.

Choosing text

Tattooing has long been enamoured with words. In the past, sailors tattooed 'hold' on the fingers of one hand, and 'fast' on the fingers of the other, so that they would never lose their grip on the riggings and lines high above deck and plunge to their death.

Political prisoners often tattooed slogans on their bodies as their only form of protest. Prisoners and gang members still tattoo powerful words on themselves as a form of identification and affiliation.

Patriotic tattoos often use text to proclaim pride in one's country. The tattoos of military service personnel are often inscribed with the names of their units, or use words to identify their branch of service.

Biblical passages, proverbs and hymns have long been very popular tattoos. Indeed, many religious texts are a rich source of material and inspiration for people who are looking for tattooed words to live by.

Buddhist texts are reminders of spiritual truths and also act as protection against evil. Even more magical are the tattoos inked by priests in Thailand. Devotees pray in preparation for the tattooing ritual of the sacred text, and may enter a state of ecstasy afterwards. These texts, beautiful in form and meaning, originate from enlightened minds, so placement on the body should be considered with care.

In India, some sects have sacred Hindu texts inscribed on every part of their bodies to protect them from harm – even inside the mouth. There are apparently no lengths to which the devoted will not go, nor limits to the expression of their true devotion.

DISPLAY CONSIDERATIONS

You will often find that tattooed text is inscribed within a ribbon or scroll to stand out, or to be worked into a larger tattoo. This is particularly true with memorial tattoos, which may also feature the names of individuals along with dates and times.

Angelina Jolie, Brandon Boyd and David Beckham carry sacred texts around with them, including the well-known 'Om mane padme om', which denotes loving kindness, purification and protection. Mantras like these are powerful, so should be correctly drawn and appropriately located, always high

> "LOVE LASTS FOREVER, A TATTOO LASTS SIX MONTHS LONGER"
>
> ANON

on the body. Proportion and construction of the characters might also be important, since the text sometimes gains power from its form, not just from its intellectual meaning.

If you are considering a sacred text, it's an idea to check out its implications. It's not appropriate, for instance, to take Koranic scriptures into the bathroom, or anywhere containing impurities. Islam also prohibits certain illustrations of living beings, but tattoo lovers have skirted the law by shaping text into animal forms – a practice called zoomorphic calligraphy.

Using foreign languages is a popular way of displaying words as body art. Japanese kanji and Chinese characters are perhaps the best-known examples, although many people choose ancient Latin or Greek, Spanish, French or Farsi.

Another way to make a passage or saying unique is in the creative and imaginative use of fonts. Some people may choose to have their family name tattooed in Olde English or a Gothic script, while others choose a more modern font.

'The alphabet is a system and series of symbols representing, collectively, the elements of written language that should be studied not only to gain the thoughts it reveals, but also to know it for itself alone as a sublime achievement of the human mind, and to savour the peculiar pleasure that is to be had from appreciating its beauty as a vehicle of thought.'

The Alphabet and Elements of Lettering,
Frederic W. Goudy, 1963

A BRIEF HISTORY OF
TEXT TATTOOS
AND ALPHABETS

LATIN ALPHABET
AND SYMBOLS

text tattoos in history

This tattooed lady appears to be tattooing Charlie Wagner in this 1930s promotional photo

In any discussion about lettering and text tattoos, it's always good to start at the beginning. And if you're going to talk about the history and roots of tattooing, or the origins of some aspect of body art, eventually you're going to talk to Chuck Eldridge at the Tattoo Archive.

Chuck is one of the pre-eminent tattoo historians and archivists in the world, and the curator of the Paul Rogers Collection at the Tattoo Archive in Winston Salem, North Carolina. In a conversation with the author, Chuck was unequivocal. 'Most tattoo artists hate doing lettering,' he said with a laugh, 'it's like maths. It's hard. The artists who like lettering are the people who probably have a knack and feel for it. The artists who are good at it usually have a gift for it.'

When I asked Chuck to elaborate, he continued with the explanation that good text tattoos are actually very technically challenging for the vast majority of tattoo artists. 'The spacing and the sizing, making it look right on the skin, are all difficult to do. Any good tattoo artist will tell you that. Plus, lettering often takes a lot of time to get right. And time is money. Most artists want to tattoo what they know and do best.'

SKILL IN PRACTICE

Through much of the twentieth century, tattoo artists in North America numbered in the mere hundreds, unlike the thousands who ply the trade today. Most tattoo artists had to supplement their tattooing income with other part-time jobs and skills. One of the more common sidelines to a tattoo practice was sign painting and lettering. Dave Shore, a noted tattoo artist in the Pacific Northwest, started out as a sign painter.

Chuck noted that the tattoo artists who worked the Pike at Long Beach in California – the West Coast's version of Coney Island in New York – were more accomplished than most at producing notable tattoo lettering. The Pike boasted a number of tattoo shops in a small area (as many as six), a concentration of tattoo artists that was unusual in the era following World War II, when tattoo artists were widely scattered, no more than one or two in even the largest urban centres. The reason for their overall collective skill level may have been no more complicated than the fact that their customers were requesting a large number of text tattoos and lettering. Long Beach

was a major port for the US Navy, and the Pike was filled with sailors on shore leave who lined up to get tattoos on payday. Added Chuck, 'If you tattoo enough of something, eventually you'll get good at it!'

Zeke Owens, who worked for a time in the Pike, was one of the best letterers of his generation, in Chuck's estimation. 'But those were different times, you didn't see the large text tattoos that you do now. People didn't ask for them. Most lettering was relatively small, straightforward script, and most of it was in a banner of some description.' As for the idea that there was any such thing as a tattoo typeface, or tattoo font, Chuck disputes that notion. The signage on tattoo shops themselves often emulated the graphic designs or lettering associated with circuses and sideshows, but Chuck says that kind of lettering almost never ended up transferred to the skin of clients. 'It was all pretty much the kind of lettering you see in the reproductions of Sailor Jerry's flash designs. Small neat script,' says Chuck. 'Really that was about it for lettering up until the modern era.'

DEVELOPING THE STYLE

Acclaimed tattoo artist Jack Rudy was one of the first of the modern era who gained a reputation for his lettering, and he was drawn at an early age to the tattoo scene at the Pike. Rudy was tattooed by Goodtime Charlie Cartwright there in 1969, and later apprenticed with Cartwright at Goodtime Charlie's Tattooland in East Los Angeles in the mid-1970s, not long after getting out of the Marine Corps. Rudy and Cartwright, catering to a largely Mexican-American clientele, were heavily influenced by the Latino low rider and cholo culture that surrounded the East LA shop. They evolved the unique style of tattooing that came to be known as 'black and grey.' Using single needles and small needle groupings, their style was reminiscent of work in prisons, where inmates tattooed using guitar strings as needles in homemade tattoo machines, and where the absence of colour was dictated by the restrictions imposed by a life behind bars.

Rudy and Cartwright's fine-line, single-needle style lent itself to the script lettering that was, and continues to be, popular among Latinos in Southern California. The Latino culture also provided them with an incredibly rich vein of symbols and designs to mine; images that drew heavily on Roman Catholic iconography and symbols that were epitomised by roses, rosary beads and images of the Virgin of Guadalupe (the Mexican Virgin Mary). The embrace of this new style by established artists gave the work a profile and credibility that might otherwise have taken much longer to achieve.

Rudy had been fascinated by lettering at an early age, and remembers practising his penmanship and copying comic-book art by the time he was in his early teens. Rudy cites Greg Irons (a highly respected and innovative underground comic-book artist) and Rick Griffin as the two major influences on his lettering style, and Freddy Negrette on

> 'THIRTY YEARS AGO, WHEN I FIRST STARTED, THERE WERE NO TATTOO MAGS, NO CONVENTIONS WHATSOEVER'
>
> JACK RUDY, 2005

his well-known script style. The graceful, elongated script style that Rudy pioneered was unique in another respect. At that time the vast majority of clients getting tattoos were male. And men gravitated towards big, bold, colourful tattoo designs with heavy black outlining. Tattoo artists even coined the phrase, 'Big and bold so it will hold', an allusion to the fact that heavy outlining ensured a tattoo would last for decades without fading. The advent of the women's liberation movement in the late 1960s and early 1970s, and Lyle Tuttle's headline-grabbing tattooing of Janis Joplin in San Francisco, meant that more women began to get tattoos as a form

> **'I WANTED SOME DECORATION'**
>
> JANIS JOPLIN, 1968

of self-expression and independence. Rudy's fine-line style, with its delicacy and subtle shading, was tailor-made for beautiful, feminine tattoos that had enormous appeal to women, whether in black and grey or colour.

LOOKING FORWARDS

As tattoo artists like Jack Rudy, Ed Hardy, Mike Malone and others pushed the technical and artistic boundaries of body art, tattooing began to attract a new generation of artists who had backgrounds in art, graphic design and formal art school training and, in many cases, a close familiarity with typography. Text tattoos were never going to be the same again.

THE LATIN ALPHABET AND ITS SYMBOLS

The development of mankind's earliest symbols into letters to represent sounds was a journey both gradual and haphazard. Eventually the phonetic alphabet was born, and allowed Western thought and culture to blossom.

This alphabet is known either as the Latin alphabet or the Roman alphabet, and is the most widely used alphabetic writing system in the world. Its origins can be traced back to the first primitive impressions painted on the walls of caves.

An alphabet of abstract symbols is an entirely different concept from a pictographic writing system, such as the Egyptian hieroglyphs or the earliest Chinese characters. It was from such pictographic systems, however, that all phonetic systems evolved. Those early pictorial representations of things and ideas morphed, over time, into simpler symbols (letters) that were, in themselves, meaningless, yet, when sequenced together, acquired meaning as words.

ANCIENT HISTORY

At least as far back as 1700 BCE, a Semitic people working in Egypt brought the concept of pictographic writing to their homeland in the Near East. Unlike the thousands of hieroglyphic symbols used by the Egyptians, the Semitic tribe required only 22 symbols to represent their consonants. The nearby Canaanites, Hebrews and Phoenicians all adapted this consonants-only alphabet, but it was the Phoenicians whose redesign of the script over centuries proved most user-friendly. As successful traders, they travelled widely from their homeland (now Lebanon), spreading their alphabet throughout the lands of the Mediterranean and Asia Minor.

Around 1000 BCE, the Greeks adopted the Phoenician alphabet,

A SHORT GLOSSARY OF TERMS

Abjads – a consonants only alphabet that emerged
in the Near East 4,000 years ago.
Etruscan – a form of the Greek alphabet that the Romans
altered to become the language we have today.
Fricative consonents – formed by forcing air through a narrow
channel in the mouth eg the letter 'f' or the last consonent in 'Bach'.
Glottal-stop – a non sound in an alphabet, eg the hyphen in 'uh-oh'.
Phoenicians – the first state-level society to
make extensive use of the alphabet.

added vowels and created a truly phonetic alphabet. They named this the alphabet, derived from its first two letters, alpha and beta.

The Romans embraced a subsequent version of the Greek alphabet, the Etruscan alphabet, then altered it to suit their special linguistic needs. Roman imperialism was responsible for spreading the alphabet throughout Western Europe, and when the Empire collapsed in the fifth century CE, the looting barbarians didn't realise that their most precious spoil of war was the alphabet they would use to write their own language. Today, the Latin alphabet is the writing system used by thousands of languages around the world.

THE LETTERS

An 'A' indicates that a student has done well in their studies, an 'F' is not so good. An 'L' warns of a novice behind the wheel of the car, and, of course, 'X' marks the spot. A look back at the derivation of the Latin letters reveals many similarities with the letters of the Phoenician alphabet.

THE LETTER A

In *abjads* the letter 'A' stood for *aleph*, signifying the ox, the most important animal in many early cultures. Its sound was a glottal stop which the Greeks felt they didn't need, and so used the vacancy to introduce their first vowel, alpha. The Romans just called it 'A'.

The letter B

In Phoenician script, the letter signified *beth*, meaning 'house' (or 'place', 'temple', 'woman' or 'daughter'). It was possibly derived from an Egyptian hieroglyph meant to depict a reed hut, and standing for an 'h' sound. To the Greeks it became beta, and to the Romans, 'B'.

The letter C

The Phoenicians called it *gimel*, signifying the camel, the carrier, without which one couldn't communicate between one oasis and another. To the Greeks it became gamma. The Etruscans had no familiarity with the 'g' sound, so they sounded it as 'k'. It was the Romans who made use of it as the letter 'C'. By adding a serious serif, they had another letter, 'G'.

The letter D

Known by the Phoenicians as *daleth*, the 'door'. The two triangles look like a fish. The Greeks called it delta, and of course it's now our 'D'.

The letter E

Before the Greeks called this letter epsilon, the Phoenicians called it *he*. It was an 'E' all right, although it appeared backwards. In its earliest incarnation the 'E' looked like a man with his arms raised. In the English language, it's the most commonly used letter.

The letter F

This started life as the Phoenician *waw*, resembling a hook, which the Etruscans used as their 'V' before handing it off to the Romans as their 'F'.

The letter H

Heth to the Phoenicians traces back to the Egyptian hieroglyphic system, and looks like a fence. Technically, it's a voiceless glottal fricative. The Greeks knew it as eta, and the Romans turned it into our 'H'.

The letters I and J

The 'hand' was originally the whole arm, simplified by the Greeks to become their iota, before the Romans made good use of it, not only as their 'I' but as their Roman numeral, uno. With a slight 'bending of the arm', they also made a 'J' out of it.

The letter K

In its earliest mode it represented the palm of the hand, then appeared as a backward 'K' in Phoenician hands. The Greeks turned it the other direction to serve as their kappa, for the Romans, the 'K'. With three letters representing the 'k' sound – 'C', 'K' and 'Q' – the Romans favoured the 'C', saving the 'K' for foreign words.

The letter L

From the Phoenician *lamedh* to the Greek lambda, it started life as a shepherd's staff, or more probably an ox goad. It turned (upside down) by the time it became the Roman 'L'.

The letter M

A zigzag wave symbol in its earliest form, it was called *mem* in Phoenician, then mu when it reached Greece. The Romans preserved it as the letter 'M'.

The letter N

If fish doesn't come to mind, then think eel or snake. An angular version of the snaking line becomes nu for the Greeks, and for the Romans, 'N'.

The letter O

Originally oval, *ayin* was the eye. In the Phoenician alphabet it had a rounder shape, and was voiced as one of those deep, throaty sounds. The Greeks used it as their small 'o', employing the omega as the big one. The Romans didn't mess with the perfection of 'O'.

The letter P

Pe, the Phoenician symbol for mouth, didn't much resemble one, so the Greeks put it to work as their symbol for pi, which, of course, became the Roman letter 'P'. Many English words that begin with 'ph' have their origins in the Greek letter phi.

The letter Q

Looking like a lollipop on a stick, *qoph*, meaning 'monkey', may have actually been the symbol for a knot. In either case, it called up a guttural 'k'-like sound. The Greeks adopted this 'Q', but their preference lay with the kappa. Western Greeks hung on to it long enough for the Romans to pick it up and use it only before a 'u'. The English language still follows that convention.

THE LETTER R

From an early symbol for the head, the Greeks made a 'P' out of it. The Romans, already having one, added an extra leg to invent the letter 'R'.

THE LETTER S

What started life as a symbol for tooth became for the Phoenicians something that resembled our 'W', but which the Greeks applied to their notion of sigma. It's not far from the angular sigma to the rounded Roman 'S'. In English, the letter 'S' begins more words than any other letter in the alphabet.

THE LETTER T

Originally an 'X' mark, the Greeks put it to use as their mark for tau, and the Romans for the letter 'T'.

THE LETTERS U, V AND Y

The *waw* sign, which gave us (in typically circuitous fashion) our 'F', was also the inspiration behind the Greek upsilon, which became the Roman letter 'Y', and subsequently our fifth vowel, as well as a consonant. From the upsilon also sprang the Roman 'V', used as both consonant and the 'u' vowel sound. Later, it would appear as the written letter 'U', the two being interchangeable until relatively recent times.

THE LETTER W

Our 'W' wasn't devised until the seventh century CE, when, in the aftermath of the Anglo Saxon invasion of Britain, the runic alphabet was the operative writing system. Monks labouring in their scriptoria tried to incorporate the Latin alphabet. One vestige is two 'U's (or 'V's) combined as one letter, the 'W'.

THE LETTER X

This obvious sign started out looking more like a telephone pole with three horizontals. It was called *samekh* and signified fish. The Greeks inherited it and used it for their xei, which sounded like 'ks'. They also created a variation of it for their letter chi, which is the 'X' version adopted by the Romans. The least-used letter in the English language, 'X' is nevertheless a powerful symbol much used in advertising. We use it to mark a ballot, and it is the mark or 'signature' of illiterate people around the world.

THE LETTER Z

Zayin is believed to have represented a weapon of some kind, perhaps even the Zorro-esque sword. It became the Greek zeta. The Romans didn't use this 'Z' until they embraced it as a means of including some Greek words into their lexicon, in the first century CE.

TWO CASES

An alphabet that has both upper- and lowercase letters, such as the Latin alphabet, is known as a bicameral alphabet. Not all alphabets have such a feature – Hebrew, for example, does not.

NUMBERS

Numbers are potentially intriguing tattoo elements. Who, in a moment of truth, won't confess to harbouring a number they consider lucky? Some numbers are especially and profoundly important to us; the birthdays and anniversaries of loved ones, for example or the date of passing of a dearly departed.

The numbers that we call Arabic numerals are referred to as Hindu numerals by Arabs, and in fact this is where the copyright belongs, with Indian mathematicians living around CE 500. Arabs get the credit because it was from North Africa that medieval Europeans first encountered these characters, which have formed the basis of our number system, roughly since Gutenberg invented his moveable type (1450s).

Of course before the numerals were set down, people were already counting. Fingers and thumbs were certainly the first abacus, making the decimal system, based on 10, an inevitable invention. The earliest evidence of a counting system comes from Egypt and involves repeated signs for one, up to the count of 10, then a repeated sign for each group of 10. Roman numerals are a classic example of this system. However it was the 'Arabic' system of numerals that emerged the victor. From its ancient Brahmi origins, to Hindu, then to Arabic and through medieval to modern times, the organic growth of the numerals, zero to nine, can be visibly traced.

Many numbers beyond the single digits have well-known cultural significance, such as 13. You're not likely to find the unluckiest number on racing cars, stable doors or athletes' jerseys. In medieval times, witches in Europe were believed to have supernatural powers associated with the cycles of the moon, precisely 13 in a year. For many religions, the number 13 has positive associations, such as rebirth in Christianity, mercy in Judaism and remembrance of God in Sikhism.

Tattoos can symbolise anything from gang membership to years spent behind bars

Religions and cults in general abound with mystical and magical numbers, such as the devilish 666. Then, just when you think you're numerologically safe, new research on ancient manuscripts lets 666 off the hook, and suggests that you now might want to beware of 616.

There's even something called the 'Jesus number', 153, derived from the numerological value for the phrase 'my Son is the God'. What do you get when you add the Jesus number to 777 (the numerological value for the word 'cross')?
The sum is 930, which equals the value of 'peace'.

Football star David Beckham shows his combination of graphic, alphabet and numerical tattoos on his arm

While the symbols are unencumbered by historical meaning beyond their numerical value, various traditions have since cloaked the numerals with esoteric significance. From Pythagoras to pure hokum, our numbers have been alchemised into concepts to either fear or revere. Saint Augustine of Hippo (CE 354–430), for instance, is quoted as saying, 'Numbers are the universal language offered by the deity to humans as confirmation of the truth'.

Diverse meanings have been ascribed to our basic numbers by various traditions, from numerology to the tarot, to sheer superstition.

1	*The beginning and the end, the alpha and omega. Pure potential. Or, it can mean total failure. Yang energy. Positivity and free will. Number one is often used to denote oneself, as in, 'I'm taking care of number one.' One is the first, the best and the only. It has no divisors, no factors, no components. It stands for independence and the individual, or God.*
2	*Yin energy. Balance and union. Duality and opposition. Two gets complicated because it beckons us to choose. If one is the essence then two is the existence. In Cantonese numerology, this number means 'easy'. In poker, the lowly deuce is sometimes wild, sometimes king.*
3	*Neutrality. Mystery and initiation. Two is linear, three is geometric. Three dimensions create the solid contents of life. Aspects of life and spirituality seem to come in threes: the Holy Trinities in many religions; the past, present and future; thought, word and deed; animal, vegetable, mineral; me, myself and I; and, perhaps most importantly, God is omniscient, omnipresent and omnipotent.*
4	*Creation, stability, simplicity and practicality. Think achievement and humility. Four speaks of being calm and grounded. The centre of the cyclone. Four is square and natural, solid and whole. The four seasons, four cardinal directions, four elements in nature. At the core of Buddhist teaching are the Four Noble Truths (life is suffering; it has a cause; an end to suffering is possible; the way out is the Noble Eightfold Path). In Chinese numerology four is unlucky, being a homonym with the word for death.*
5	*Five fingers, five toes, five senses – the number five is physical. Action and adventure. Restlessness, passion and unpredictability. To the Chinese, it symbolises myself, or the concept of never. The psychologist Carl Jung saw five as the union of the first male and female numbers, hence the symbol of creative life and erotic love.*

6	*The Chinese number six means 'easy and smooth all the way'. Things unfolding as they should. Natural reactions and responsibilities. Protective and dependable, the number six is a caring number, a number that encourages us to accept what is inevitable, giving rise to compassion and forgiveness. The theory of six degrees of separation says that no one lies outside the number six.*
7	*Lucky seven. The seven deadly sins. Seven is said to represent the focused search for esoteric meaning, and is concerned with mysticism and healing. In therapeutic circles it implies thought, awareness and imagination in the service of manifesting what we want. The word Sabbath comes from the Hebrew root word for seven, meaning 'to be complete or full'. The Cantonese word for seven is considered vulgar.*
8	*Infinity. Sudden fortune, prosperity. Sacrifice and power. Opportunity. In Chinese culture, where the spoken eight sounds like 'prosper', it's considered a lucky number. It represents the totality of the universe. The Summer Olympics in Beijing commenced at 8:08 pm on August 8, 2008. Buddha taught his Noble Eightfold Path. And finally, 'He that is eight days old shall be circumcised among you...'*
9	*Symbolic of completeness because no other single digit has a higher value. Nine also symbolises vision, intellectual power, attainment and seeing the big picture. Nine months mark the human gestation period. Dante's* Inferno *speaks of nine circles of Hell and nine spheres of Heaven. The Chinese Netherworld is described as having nine rivers. In Norse mythology, secrets are revealed to Odin after hanging on the World Tree for nine nights.*

AND THE @ SIGN

Every new typeface includes three beguiling signs that are neither numbers nor letters. While they're not exactly part of the alphabet, the asterisk, ampersand and @ sign are essential elements of any font.

The ampersand (&), meaning 'and', comes to us from Latin, which, long ago, made a ligature (a marriage) out of et, the Latin for 'and'. The earliest examples of the ampersand date back to the first century CE. After centuries of rushed writing and the urge to abbreviate, the ampersand came to resemble an ambitious, rather overzealous letter 'S', but in some fonts, depending on the grandiosity of the design, the Latin et can be still be discerned.

The convention in English and French is to allow the ampersand to appear without restriction in conventional text, but German rules dictate that it be restricted to formal use, as in corporate titles that may use, as in corporate titles that may be comprised of two names, such as Schmidt & Schmidt.

The asterisk (*) – sometimes referred to as a 'star' by mathematicians and computer scientists – is constructed of three crossed lines, usually superscripted, and often of a smaller pica or point value. It has various uses, including calling out a footnote, or denoting a wildcard, repetition or multiplication. Multiple asterisks are used to blot out letters of a word that might offend. This versatile little glyph can serve as bullets in a list, or assume a value, for example when reviewing and rating movies.

Then there's the @. English speakers call it the 'at' sign, while Italians call it a 'snail', and some Slavs refer to it as a 'monkey'. Apparently, it has come down to us from the world of commerce, where it has long been used as shorthand to stand in for the phrase 'at the price of'. A handwritten letter exists in which a Florentine merchant made use of an @ sign in 1536. Many years later in 1971, Ray Tomlinson, the engineer who devised the first e-mail, incorporated the @ in the destination address.

INFINITY SYMBOL

Infinity, according to mathematics, is an unimaginably large value, and the English mathematician John Wallis gets the credit for first using this symbol to signify infinity in his *Arithmetica Infinitorum* of 1655. He may have derived it from a symbol that served the Romans to signify 1,000 or 'many'. More likely, the infinity symbol was a creative version of the Greek omega, the last letter of their alphabet. Speculators have focused on the lowercase omega, since, with minimal help from the calligrapher's plume, it becomes the familiar figure of eight lying on its side. But it's the uppercase omega that has ties to infinity, since it's a doppelganger for the Egyptian hieroglyph known as the shen-ring which, for thousands of years, has represented that which cannot be expressed by numbers.

Pi SYMBOL

The earliest known reference to pi is on a papyrus scroll from the period in Egyptian history known as the Middle Kingdom (roughly 2000–1650 BCE). But it was English mathematicians of the seventeenth century who introduced pi, the sixteenth letter of the Greek alphabet, to designate the circumference of a circle. We know it as the ratio of the circumference to the diameter – 3.14159265... Put more simply, pi is the number of times that a circle's diameter will fit around the circumference. It was William Jones who first established the usage in his *Synopsis Palmariorum Matheseos* of 1706. He thought it would serve well as a symbol for 'periphery'. It wasn't until 1737, when a mathematician named Euler adopted Jones' pi, that the practice caught on.

PER CENT SYMBOL

Although the Roman emperor Augustus had no knowledge of percentages, he levied a tax on goods sold at auction at the rate of 1/100. By the Middle Ages, one hundred had become a common reference point in business transactions. Records from fifteenth-century Italy contain references such as '20 p 100', meaning 20 per cent, and 'x p cento', or 'xx per c' signifying 10 and 20 per cent respectively. The term 'per cent', for tallying interest, profit and loss, was in common use from then on.

To trace the evolution of the symbol itself would require painstaking examination of financial documents from the fifteenth to seventeenth centuries, when the 'c' may or may not have evolved into another '0', and the horizontal vinculum (—) became the slanted solidus (/), to give the 0/0.

Ilustration showing a view of Emma de Burgh's elaborately tattooed back, on which Leonardo Da Vinci's 'Last Supper' appears as a motif. Late nineteenth-century woodcut.

ALPHABETS AND
SCRIPTS TATTOO
DIRECTORY

EGYPTIAN HIEROGLYPHS
VIKING RUNES GREEK
LATIN SANSKRIT PERSIAN/
FARSI HEBREW CYRILLIC/
RUSSIAN CHINESE JAPANESE
ELVISH MUSICAL NOTATION
MONOGRAMS LOGOS
AMBIGRAMS...

EGYPTIAN HIEROGLYPHS

Hieroglyphs were the symbols used to write the ancient Egyptian language. Based on simple pictures of well-known objects, the hieroglyphic writing system is one of the oldest in the world.

The Egyptians called them 'gods' words', while the Greeks, upon first seeing this colourful pictorial script in religious settings, called it *hiera grammata* ('the sacred letters'), or *hieroglyphica* ('the sacred carved letters').

It's not known what influenced the Egyptians in their choice of writing system, but it is believed that the hieroglyphs inspired later alphabets that then evolved into the Phoenician, Hebrew and Greek alphabets.

Hieroglyphs were found carved in stone in temples and the tombs of pharaohs, and so were thought to contain the kind of mystical wisdom and knowledge needed to negotiate the journey from this life to the next. However, breaking the hieroglyphic code was complicated by a Western notion that the characters in this colourful 'alphabet' were symbolic rather than phonetic. Some investigators were even convinced that each symbol represented an abstract concept that transcended language – from symbol directly to thought. Such extravagant and hyperbolic speculation cloaked the hieroglyphs in ever more mystery, which may explain why they are the chosen script for the most exotic text tattoos.

Patron of: the home, childbirth, infants, humour, song and dance.

Bes: Protector of Childbirth

Patron of: fertile lands.

Ha'py: God of the Nile river

Patron of: creation.

Harakhy (Ra): The Sun God

Patron of: rulers, law, war, young men, light and the sun.

Horus: King of the Gods on Earth

Patron of: the sun, creation, life and resurrection.

Khepri: The Great Scarab

Patron of: the creation of people and animals.

Khnum: The Great Potter

Patron of: mummification and the dead.

Anubis: God of Embalming

ANCIENT EGYPTIAN SCRIPTS

The hieroglyphs were a formal script reserved for monuments and religious and political edicts, while a script called 'hieratic' was the system used for everyday writing with ink on papyrus. In hieratic, pictorial representations were reduced to lines and squiggles, so they weren't true hieroglyphs. A third script, called 'demotic,' was more highly cursive – with linked letters – and served as the secular writing medium. These scripts did not migrate beyond Egypt's borders, nor did Egypt's conquerors bother to learn them, so that with the Roman invasion of 30 BCE, the future of hieroglyphs looked dim. When the Christian Emperor Theodosius closed all of Egypt's pagan temples in CE 391, the hieroglyphs were officially assigned to oblivion. The last known hieroglyphic inscription was carved into the Gate of Hadrian, sometime around CE 394.

Hieratic glyphs (above)

Demotic script (above)
Sample of Egyptian written in hieratic script (below)

BREAKING THE CODE

Much of our fascination with hieroglyphs stems from the mystery of their meaning. Until the turn of the nineteenth century there was no consensus on whether the hieroglyphs were even a proper writing system. The code was not broken until Napoleon's troops, campaigning in Egypt in 1799, discovered the Rosetta Stone, inscribed with a hieroglyphic text translated twice, once into Greek and again into a common Egyptian dialect. The hieroglyphs, it turned out, were indeed a bona fide writing system.

DECIPHERING HIEROGLYPHS

Hieroglyphs were generally written from right to left, although left to right worked just as well, as did top to bottom. The direction in which the glyphs faced – a bird looking left, for example – showed the reader how to proceed. Words weren't demarcated by spaces or punctuation, although some glyphs served as word-endings.

Two basic types of hieroglyph rendered the ancient Egyptian language into text: logograms and phonograms. Logograms stand for the object they clearly represent – an eye is an eye, for example – and these were the most frequently used common nouns. Phonograms are phonetic – representing sounds – in the style of most alphabets. Some symbols had a dual purpose: 'mouth', for instance, also represented the 'r' sound. Other signs in the system, called 'determinatives,' were mute characters located at the end of a word, which gave the reader a clue to the word's meaning. Most hieroglyphic words were comprised of phonetic signs followed by one determinative.

The hieroglyphic script had a clumsy system for numbers and no vowels, but it contained 24 symbols standing for single consonants, and these might have sufficed to construct every word in the language, had Egyptians not continued to employ hundreds of other symbols and logograms, ensuring that their writing system remained complex, never to evolve into a true alphabet.

HIEROGLYPHIC TATTOOS

As symbols, the hieroglyphs continue to be meaningful signs to many people today, particularly as a talisman or amulet, and most especially as tattoos.

ΑΠΚΗ

The pagan ankh was adopted by the Egyptian Copts as their own unique *crux ansata* ('cross with a handle'). It became the crucifix symbol of the Coptic church, representing the hope of future life and resurrection, and at the same time acknowledging previous religions of Egypt. It came to be known as the Egyptian cross and the key of life, its keylike shape inspiring the belief that it could unlock the gates of death.

Egyptologists still puzzle over the ankh's precise origins, since it's a hybrid of two nearly universal symbols. The loop suggests the sunrise, the sun rising over the horizon – the crossbar – with the vertical line representing the path of the sun. One theory holds that it represents the gods Osiris and Isis, male and female. The cross and circle represent the union of heaven and earth. The ankh also symbolised the water used in purification rituals, and metal mirrors were occasionally ankh-shaped, perhaps to reflect the belief that life and death mirror each other. With so many associations, it's not surprising that it's a favoured tattoo charm.

EYE OF HORUS

Horus, also known as Ra, the sky god, had the head of a falcon and was attributed with qualities of light and goodness. Amulets in the shape of his eye were often found in royal tombs for protection in the afterlife. The eye also signified royal power. The ancients believed it to be a symbol of indestructibility that would assist in rebirth, which is perhaps why it was found under the twelfth layer of bandages on Tutankhamen's mummy.

The more recent tradition of freemasonry adopted the symbol, as did the United States as an element on its Great Seal, where it appears on the reverse side atop a pyramid as the eye of providence. The eye of Horus also shows up in Buddhism as the eye of the world, implying the enlightened perspective of Buddha himself. Ancient sailors in the Mediterranean region were said to have painted the eye on their vessel's bow to ensure a safe voyage.

SCARAB

The scarab has found immortality as one of the favourite icons of Egyptian mythology and pseudo-Egyptian art. As a hieroglyph, this humble dung beetle represented Khepri, the Egyptian god of the rising sun and another version of the sun god, Ra. The ancients thought that male scarabs incubated their own semen in balls of dung, which they then rolled around in imitation of Khephri rolling the sun across the sky. So, in the mythology of ancient Egypt, the scarab became a symbol of genesis, rebirth and the eternal life force.

The scarab hieroglyph was often used by the pharaohs as one of their many royal titles, including that of the famous boy-king, Tutankhamen.

SERKET

This logogram is symbolic of the scorpion itself, and the goddess Serket, one of four goddesses who protected coffins. As an element of hieroglyphic text, this character was used as an unvoiced determinative, suggesting 'to breathe', or 'to sniff the wind'. The image was also put to work on Egyptian amulets for protection and healing power against scorpion stings and snake bites.

SHEN-RING

Like the modern-day infinity sign, the shen-ring hieroglyph represents 'that which cannot be expressed by numbers'. A circle with a straight line running tangentially to its bottom edge, the shen-ring signified a looped rope with the excess at each end sticking out horizontally. The symbol perfectly represented ancient Egypt's dual concept of time, the circle suggesting cyclical events, such as the flooding of the Nile, and the straight line heading to eternity. Other meanings included 'all that the sun surrounds', and 'protection from the all-surrounding chaos'.

The shen-ring's protective power was employed as a cartouche to encircle the names of royalty, the shape being elongated to accommodate the many titles in the pharaoh's name.

VIKING RUNES

An alphabet of runes existed among northern Germanic tribes long before the Viking age began, but it was the Scandinavian Vikings who, towards the end of the first millennium, left the most lasting and potent evidence of this angular set of symbols.

The Vikings carved runes most often on rocks, inscriptions that hinted at heroic exploits and famous people. Runes eventually came into use as an oracular device to consult about matters both public and personal. The use of runes ended in the Middle Ages, when the medieval Church outlawed them in an effort to stamp out paganism and drive the Devil out of Europe. The current popularity of runes as a form of tattoo script is due to precisely those outlawed occult activities – as a medium of divination and magic. However sincerely we play with the ancient runes, we should be aware that very little is actually known about them.

FUTHARK

The runic alphabet is called 'futhark', and takes its name from the first six letters of the runic sequence: fehu; uruz; thurisaz; ansuz; raido and kenaz. While most alphabets employ letters that are meaningless beyond the phonetic sound they represent, each rune is a word that may also have a special meaning associated with Norse mythology. Fehu, for example, means 'cattle'. The futhark originally consisted of 24 letters (the 'elder' futhark, shown below), but was reduced to 16 characters.

This unorthodox alphabet was eventually displaced in Europe by the Latin alphabet, yet the runes survived in manuscripts and as inscriptions in stone, wood, horn and metal.

ᚠ	Ansuz	'god'
ᛒ	Berkanan	'birth tree'
ᚦ	Burisaz	'Thor'
ᛞ	Dagaz	'day'
ᛗ	Ehwaz	'horse'
ᚠ	Fehu	'wealth/cattle'
ᚷ	Gebo	'gift'
ᚺ	Hagalaz	'hail'
ᛁ	Isaz	'ice'

⏉	Jera	'year'
⟨	Kaunan	'torch'
⍓	Laguz	'water'
ᛗ	Mamaz	'man'
ᚾ	Naudiz	'need'
ᛟ	Obila	'heritage'
ᛈ	Perb	'pear tree'
ᚱ	Raido	'ride'
ᛋ	Sonilo	'sun'
T	Tiwaz	'Tyr'
ᚢ	Uruz	'auroch'
ᛜ	Ingwaz	'Yngvi'
ᚹ	Wungo	'joy'
ᛖ	Ehwaz	'yew tree'
ᛉ	Algiz	'elk'

SPIRITUAL CONNECTION

The process of writing with runes is seen by its serious practitioners as a magical act. Perhaps more than any other alphabet, the runes transmit, to those who believe in them, an understanding of the sensibilities of the ancients who devised them. The runes speak of a special connection to the natural world, a large part of which is the spirit world.

It is not clear when the runes first came into use, nor where they came from, although the earliest-found runes date back to the second and third centuries CE. That the runes grew from some previous alphabet is generally agreed, although whether that alphabet was Latin, Greek or Etruscan is not known. Even the Gokturks, the first Turks, wrote their language in a runic script, and pre-runic symbols have been found in Bronze Age rock carvings. However, Scandinavians speak of their runes as gifts from their chief god, Odin. With such a divine origin, it's no wonder that Nordic peoples have so revered the runes, and attributed to them magical powers.

Thor

God of Thunder

Tyr

God of Combat

ᛒᚱᚢᚦᚢᚱ

Brother

ᚠᚨᚦᚢᚱ

Father

ODIN'S RUNE SONG

I know that I hung on a windy tree
nine long nights,
wounded with a spear, dedicated to Odin,
myself to myself,
on that tree of which no man knows
from where its roots run.

No bread did they give me nor a drink from a horn,
downward I peered;
I took up the runes, screaming I took them,
then I fell back from there.

From Rúnatáls-tháttr-Óðins (Odin's Rune Song)

RUNESTONES

With such a strong belief in supernatural powers, the Vikings left it to a 'rune master' to negotiate the talismanic properties of their alphabet. Power is believed to infuse the arrangement of lines of a single rune. Consulting the runes for guidance was an art not taken lightly. 'Let no man carve runes to cast a spell', said a Viking poet, 'save first he learns to read them well'. Viking legends speak of health and illness, and of luck and disaster that flow from the right or wrong runic combinations or spellings. For this reason, spiritualists would warn against taking on a runic tattoo without proper consideration.

When the Vikings voyaged across the seas, they naturally took their system of writing with them, leaving runic inscriptions on everything from stone monoliths to household tools. Large freestanding rocks called runestones were often raised as memorials to the dead, inscribed with both religious and practical information. Some of the best inscriptions comprise a list of the entire runic alphabet. Rune poems from the ninth to the twelfth centuries CE explain the runes one by one, a verse dedicated to each rune. However, any knowledge that rune masters might have had has long vanished in the mists of time. The modern-day rune revival owes much of its success to apocryphal nonsense dispensed by self-awareness gurus.

INTERPRETATION

While we entertain ourselves with the runes – even tattooing them on our bodies – it should be remembered that they emerged from a society fundamentally different from our own. While we may deploy them for purposes of protection, personal therapy and fortune telling, the most conscientious among us will not lose sight of the fact that they reflect the ancient Norse world-view. The interpretations of the runes we read about in New Age books are unlikely to resemble the true and original meanings of the runes.

†HE GREEK ALPHABE†

The Greek alphabet emerged at about the time the ancient Olympic Games first came into play, circa 700 BCE. This alphabet distinguished itself from others by becoming the first writing system with a separate symbol for every sound, including vowels along with the consonants, and featured upper and lower cases.

The Greek alphabet arose – in reality it was a sophisticated adaptation – from the lettering system used by the Phoenician culture, which at the time was the unrivalled economic and maritime power of the Mediterranean basin. The new Greek alphabet in turn gave rise to the Cyrillic, Gothic, Coptic and Latin alphabets, and was converted into the most sophisticated writing apparatus ever known. By including vowels as well as consonants, this purely phonetic alphabet became the basis of all modern Western alphabets.

Originally, the Greek alphabet was written right to left, but later was reversed and has remained so ever since. The two main variants of the ancient Greek alphabet are the Latin alphabet and the Greek one we see today.

Α Ά Β Γ Δ Ε Έ Ζ Η Ή

Θ Ό Ι Ί Ϊ Κ Λ Μ Ν Ξ Ο Π

Ρ Σ Τ Υ Ύ Ϋ Φ Χ Ψ Ω Ώ

α ά β γ δ ε έ ζ ή θ ι ί

ϊ ΐ κ λ μ ν ξ ο ό π ρ σ τ

υ ύ ϋ ΰ φ χ ψ ω ώ

DİPHTHODGS

ει	εῖ
υι	υῖ
αι	αῖ
υι	ου
εϊ	οϋ
υϊ	οὖ
αϊ	

GREEK SYMBOLS TODAY

Through the ages, scholars, mathematicians, scientists and astronomers have used specific letters from this alphabet as symbols in their work and research. Physics uses the letter λ (lambda), for example, to mean 'wavelength', while the Greek letter ω (omega) represents 'ohms', a measure of electrical resistance. Computer users will be familiar with the symbol Σ (sigma) appearing in the toolbar of Microsoft Excel, which represents a 'sum'. These letters-as-symbols have, over time, entered the general lexicon.

GREEK-LETTER SOCIETIES

In the late eighteenth century, university students were steeped in the classics and were familiar with Greek and Latin, indeed a classic liberal arts education in the humanities included studying both Greek and Latin literary classics in their original language. An educated man – or the rare woman – would have been conversant with Homer's *Odyssey* in the original Greek.

These students, being as romantic and as steeped in poetry then as they are now, took certain Greek letters to identify secret societies within their universities and colleges. The letters of the Greek alphabet came to represent a particular fraternity within the place of learning. Many of these societies, particularly in North America, were created in order to discuss topics beyond the conservative curriculum and, along with their love of learning, they adopted codes of high ethical conduct, secret rituals, oaths and membership badges.

Fraternities – and later sororities for women – are still very much alive in colleges and universities today, all proudly sporting the Greek letter of their society. Among the brothers and sisters of many fraternities and sororities, getting a Greek-letter tattoo is as much a rite of passage and a ritual as the 'secret handshake' that identifies fellow members.

αντρία
courage

ελευθερία
freedom

γενναιότητα
bravery

THE LATIN ALPHABET

For a 'dead' language, Latin is still making a lot of noise. It's alive in those useful little phrases in scientific and legal documents, as the mottoes of learned institutions, on clan crests and more recently as a growing trend in text tattoos.

Angelina Jolie covered up a dragon tattoo on her abdomen with a cross and the Latin phrase, *Quod me netrit me destruit*, meaning, 'What nourishes me also destroys me'. Football legend David Beckham commissioned a Latin text tattoo in conjunction with his wife's name. It reads, *Ut amem et foveam*, which translates as, 'So that I love and cherish'.

Any foreign-language tattoo comes with the nuisance factor of having to continuously explain it. Furthermore, a simple translation may only whet a person's curiosity. An enthusiastic and responsible tattoo host will be able to regale a questioner with facts concerning the birth of the Latin language, its development and especially its dogged determination not to be entirely lost in the mists of time.

A B C D E F G H I K L M

N O P Q R S T V X Y Z

a b c d e f g h i k l m

n o p q u r s t v x y z

. , & ! ? $ £ ß ƒ @ π µ ©

THE LATIN ALPHABET

In the eighth century BCE, Latin was spoken by tribes in the vicinity of present-day Rome. However, there would be no written language until the seventh century BCE, when the Romans successfully borrowed an alphabet from the nearby Etruscans. The letters in these early writing systems resembled the angular characters of the familiar Viking runes, and they served the Romans well as a means of writing their spoken Latin. The earliest evidence of written Latin is an obscure inscription on a pin that dates to the sixth century BCE, and little more has been discovered that predates the third century BCE.

The Latin alphabet – also known as the Roman alphabet – was soon obliged to borrow the letters 'Y' and 'Z' in order to accommodate useful Greek words, and that was only the beginning of Latin's flexibility, as it went on to serve as the chassis for a fleet of other languages, including the Romance languages, the Germanic, Baltic and Celtic languages, indeed, most of the languages of Europe.

alis grave nil
nothing is heavy to those who have wings

temet nosce
know thyself

vive ut vivas
live so that you may live

carpe noctem
seize the night

non ducor duco
I am not lead; I lead

THE LATIN LANGUAGE

Early Latin developed a dialect that served the educated classes, but this classical Latin was lost on the common folk since they continued to speak what is known as 'vulgar Latin'. This vernacular differed from classical Latin, not only grammatically, but also in vocabulary and pronunciation. With the expansion of the Roman Empire (250–100 BCE), Latin spread throughout the Mediterranean region, its various splinters evolving eventually into the Romance languages, such as French, Spanish, Italian, Portuguese and Romanian.

Latin continued to be the sole written script, becoming the international language of science and scholarship in much of Europe. While Cicero, Virgil and Tacitus were putting Latin on the literary map – and Ovid was penning a self-help book on how to pick up women at the Forum – their stodgy classical Latin was getting left behind by vulgar Latin, which kept changing with the times.

By the eighth century CE, Latin had become a dead language, spoken in the West by few people other than monks who toiled over their handwritten manuscripts. The Catholic Church proved to be Latin's main salvation, protecting the spoken language into medieval times. Indeed, it was only in the mid-1960s that the Catholic liturgy could be read in a language other than Latin. However, the Catholic Church is the largest organisation still to use Latin, and the language remains the official tongue of the central government of the Catholic Church, the Holy See.

To this day, the Italian school system offers its high-school students Latin as a mandatory subject, although the object isn't to make Latin speakers of the Italian population, but rather to enable them to translate Latin texts into modern languages. An international 'Living Latin' movement has been attempting to resuscitate Latin for over 50 years. The Vatican offers courses in spoken Latin, as does the University of Kentucky in the US, and the Classical Association in the UK.

MODERN USES

Today, we encounter Latin most often within the disciplines of science and law, where unambiguous comprehension across language barriers is critical. Scientific nomenclature for genus and species is a good example. Legal terms such as 'a priori', 'bona fide', 'de facto' and 'habeas corpus' are familiar terms around the world. Cinema occasionally deploys Latin for the sake of authenticity, as Mel Gibson did in his *Passion of the Christ*.

Latin mottoes hold a place in the hearts of many, whether the old school slogan or the motto carried by the American eagle on its official seal: *E pluribus unum* ('Out of many, one').

American writer John Steinbeck identified himself with the motto on his personal stamp, which read, *Ad astra per alia porci*, meaning, 'To the stars on the wings of a pig'.

credo quia absurdum est
I believe it because it is absurd

alis volat propriis
she flies with her own wings

cogito ergo sum
I think therefore I am

verba volant, scripta manent
words fly away, writings remain

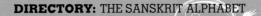

THE SANSKRIT ALPHABET

Sanskrit, from a word meaning 'refined' or 'purified', seems to generate clarity and inspiration, which would account for the explosion of creative expression that occurred wherever it was spoken in ancient times.

Constructed of primordial sounds, the language, as it developed, took into consideration the way the mouth naturally wants to sequence those sounds. For this and other reasons, Sanskrit is said to be the most systematic language in the world. Its power of expression is evidenced by the 65 words available to describe 'earth', the 67 words for 'water', and the 250 ways to say 'rainfall'.

Sanskrit descends – as most languages do – from that long-ago tongue known only as the Proto-Indo-European language, belonging to the Indo-Iranian branch of that language tree, and further, to the Indo-Aryan subfamily.

As important as Latin and Greek are to a study of most Western languages, so too is Sanskrit to a host of Indian dialects. It's been called 'the mother of all languages', which, although not true, reveals a reverence for this classical tongue. In its glory days, the 'sacred' Sanskrit was the language of all cultured people within Indian hegemony. All learning was conducted in the Sanskrit language, including translations from foreign tongues, so the vast majority of ancient documents on hand today are written in Sanskrit.

शुद्ध

peace

शुद्धः

śuddhaḥ (m)

शुद्धा

śuddhā (f)

शान्त

peaceful

शान्तः

śāntaḥ (m)

शान्ता

śāntā (f)

रम्य

delightful

रम्यः

ramyaḥ (m)

रम्या

ramyā (f)

धर्मः

dharmaḥ

virtue

विवेकः

vivekaḥ

wisdom

मुक्तिः

muktiḥ

freedom

ॐ ॐ

ॐ ॐ

om design variations

CLARITY

Sanskrit remains the liturgical language in Hindu, Buddhist and Jain rituals – mostly as hymns and mantras. Ancient Indians attached great importance to sound, bringing rhythm to their prose and musical qualities to their poetry and prayers. Sanskrit mantras are constructed of vibrations that can potentially 'open the third eye' to a perspective on reality that's closer to true objectivity, the essence of spirituality.

Sanskrit's capacity to express and investigate spiritual matters has long been taken for granted. NASA, the advanced research centre, has suggested a reason why – it's the only unambiguous language on the planet. 'In ancient India', says NASA researcher Rick Briggs, 'the intention to discover truth was so consuming, that in the process they discovered perhaps the most perfect tool for fulfilling such a search – the Sanskrit language'.

SPIRITUAL SYMBOLS

The appeal of Sanskrit tattoos is decidedly spiritual. Poignant Sanskrit quotes, reflecting expansive personal philosophies, are sourced from Buddhism, Hinduism and other Eastern disciplines, while the fact that Sanskrit is written in verse form lends it added artistry.

The most popular Sanskrit tattoo is the symbol 'om', the world's most widely recognized sacred syllable. In the Hindu dharma there is no symbol more important, since it represents 'absolute reality' (Brahman), and embodies the essence of the universe. At birth, a child born into a Hindu family has the om sign written in honey on its tongue. It appears in every Hindu temple and in the most humble of family shrines. For the devout Hindu, om is the sound uttered at the beginning of each day and before commencing any journey, great or small. It is placed at the beginning and end of most Hindu texts as a sacred exclamation. Prayers and mantras are framed by the same intonation. In fact, om is the essence of all mantras and sacred words. Little wonder that it appears on letterheads, exam papers, on pendants worn around the neck and as one of the most appropriate spiritual tattoos.

THE PERSIAN/FARSI ALPHABET

The individual inclined letters of the Persian (also known as Farsi) alphabet cling together artfully, making this an especially appropriate alphabet for calligraphy, poetry and tattoos.

There was a time when Persian was the language spoken by kings, poets, mystics and diplomats from Turkey to India to China. Persian was the international language. A member of the Indo-European language family, it is spoken today by over 130 million people, mostly in Iran, Afghanistan and Tajikistan.

Farsi script is also called Ta'liq, meaning 'hanging script', and is believed to have been developed by the Persians from a lesser-known Arabic script.

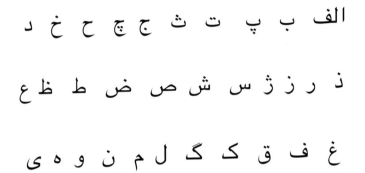

الف ب پ ت ث ج چ ح خ د

ذ ر ز ژ س ش ص ض ط ظ ع

غ ف ق ک گ ل م ن و ه ی

CALLIGRAPHY

The history of calligraphy in Persia dates back almost 3,000 years. Persian calligraphers have traditionally excelled in cursive scripts, adding ornaments and decorations and altering the letters' dimensions according to the whim of the artist and the thickness of their traditional reed pen. The most serious aficionados of Farsi claim that the form of each letter of the alphabet harmonises with a particular musical note. It's little wonder that the Persian calligraphic style was so willingly adopted by neighbouring Arabs and Indian and Turkish Muslims.

Farsi calligraphers have made an art out of manipulating the written word – a person's name, perhaps, or a poetic phrase – and morphing it to create a pleasing composition. By altering the shape of the words, calligraphers and tattooists have created traditional Persian symbols.

Farsi is beautiful enough, but when it is the medium for poetry of any of Persia's great poets – Rumi, Hafez, Saadi, Khayam – the script becomes more precious yet. Words can be arranged into patterns that suggest a flow of energy across the parchment, or human body. It is perhaps for this reason that Farsi text tattoos have such a mystical quality.

A militant from Lebanon has his arms covered in tattoos to commemorate his dead comrades

FARSI AND PARSI

'Farsi' is the Arab way of saying 'Parsi', meaning 'of Persia'. The Arabic language contains no 'p' sound, and the term Farsi predominated after Arabs invaded Iran (then known internationally as Persia, but to its people as Iran) in the seventh century AD. Many Iranians insist that their language be referred to as Persian, since Farsi conveys no hint of place or Persian history. They insist it creates confusion and misunderstanding, and that it's as incorrect as calling the Persian Gulf the Farsi Gulf. Persia-promoters point out that 'Persian' conveys not only the language but also Iran's vast cultural legacy – Persian poetry, Persian carpets, Persian cats, pistachios, cinema, architecture, etc. The word Farsi, it is argued, only adds to Iran's unfortunate reputation as an increasingly alien society.

DIRECTORY: THE PERSIAN/FARSI ALPHABET

A tattoo devotee shows off his decorated stomach during the annual tattoo fesitval in Wat Bang Phra, Thailand

THE PERSIAN LANGUAGE

Persian has influenced and been influenced by other languages. Most importantly, it is written in Arabic script, and for that reason has borrowed much from Arabic. But that's not to say that Arabs and Iranians understand each other. The average Iranian probably struggles to read the Koran, written as it is in traditional Arabic, the tongue of Mohammed. And Arabs, though they may understand most of the words in a Persian book, will be none the wiser for their failing to grasp the grammar.

Despite the common script, there seems to be a gulf between Arabic and Persian (Farsi), while much assimilation back and forth takes place between Arabic and other Semitic languages.

73

†HE HEBREW ALPHABE†

'Ye shall not make any cuttings in your flesh for the dead, nor print any marks upon you: I am the Lord'. Leviticus 19:28 notwithstanding, Hebrew is a favourite script for tattoos. The 22 letters of the alphabet are elegant, pictorial and ancient.

Hebrew is a member of the Canaanite group of Semitic languages, and is one of the longest continuously recorded languages to survive to the present day. It's an abjad writing system, meaning that it has letters for consonants only. The reader mentally fills in the appropriate vowels. A system to indicate vowels was eventually incorporated into the script, a practice called niqqud, in which dots and lines were added above or below a letter. Poetry, prayer books and foreign words were the first to get the vowel treatment, while religious texts remained true to the old ways.

Hebrew text is written horizontally from right to left, which is the first reason to consult an expert before engaging a tattooist. Also, those missing vowels can lead to misinterpretation of an isolated tattooed word devoid of context.

מ ל כ ך י

ט ח ז ו ה

ד ג ב א

ת ש ר ק

ף פ ע ס

ן נ מ

CELEBRITY FAVOURITE

The large number of celebrities sporting them on the red carpet has bolstered the popularity of Hebrew tattoos. Madonna, Britney Spears and Christina Aguilera no doubt feel empowered by taking on tattoos written in a script that has such ancient and powerful religious associations. The Beckhams – Victoria and her football-star husband David – took on matching Hebrew tattoos as a testament to their love. Their tattoos read 'I am my beloved's and my beloved is mine' – a Biblical quote from the Song of Songs. Though their tattoos have the same meaning, the text is slightly different, because Hebrew words may change according to who's speaking, male or female.

David and Victoria Beckham sport Hebrew tattoos. David's is on his left forearm (below) and Victoria has hers on the back of her neck (over page right)

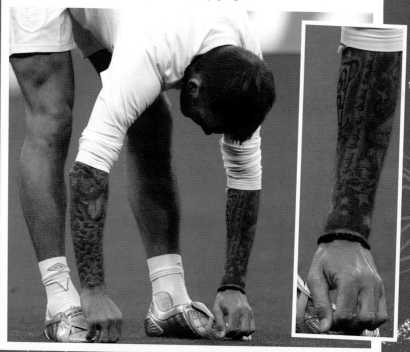

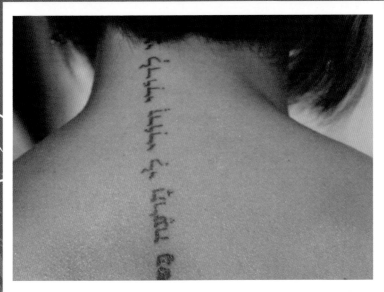

FALSE INTERPRETATIONS

Foreign-language text often presents the danger of inaccurate tattoo translation. Hebrew is especially vulnerable to faulty interpretation, especially if the desired tattoo is a slogan in a different language. 'To have and to hold' may lose its meaning when translated to Hebrew.

The Hebrew script also has special calligraphic demands. In English, an 'A' can be carelessly rendered and still be recognized as an 'A'. Not so Hebrew characters, which have precise lines, ticks, arcs, zigs and zags. If you are not a skilled linguist it can be easy to say what you don't mean. Britney Spears is reported to have had a Hebrew tattoo lasered off the back of her neck because of just such an error. She was trying to spell 'God', of which the Kabbalah suggests there are 72 variations. Or is that 72 ways to go wrong?

The word is supposed to empower the bearer, to lend her grace, strength of mind, presence of faith and, most of all, the courage to let the ego shrink to its proper place in the greater scheme of things. Deep thoughts like these are the reason why Hebrew is such a respected and sought-after tattoo script.

THE HEBREW LANGUAGE

Hebrew text dates back as far as the eleventh century BCE, when it closely resembled Aramaic. Both alphabets had the same letters in the same order, which is not surprising, considering that they had both borrowed from the Phoenician alphabet. These languages had no separate numerals, but numbers could be represented by letters. Today, of course, Hebrew speakers have recourse to the standard 1, 2, 3, etc.

By the sixth century BCE, Aramaic had established itself as the international trade language in the Middle East, so Hebrews adopted it for their common discourse, calling it 'square script', or 'Jewish script'. Old Hebrew survived as a liturgical language, and even as the spoken vernacular in a few conservative quarters. Then, around the turn of the twentieth century, the Zionist movement pushed to re-establish Hebrew as a spoken language, and in 1948 it became the official tongue of Israel, where, today, over five million people speak what's called Modern Israeli Hebrew. Around the world, another three million people are speaking this ancient language.

While we're concerned more with Hebrew script than with the development of offshoots of the spoken language, it's interesting to note how Jewish communities, wherever they were around the world – in Europe, West Asia and North Africa – managed to preserve and protect older Hebrew vocabulary and linguistic structures in whatever language they were speaking. Yiddish is the best example, the most widely spoken of all the Jewish languages, derived from medieval German dialects. Ladino is another language in the Jewish diaspora, spoken by the Sephardic Jews in Spain and Portugal. And Judaeo-Arabic is yet another.

אֲנִי

I am

מַזָּל וְהַצְלָחָה תומכים אמיץ

Fortune favours the brave

אני לדודי ודודי לי

I am my beloved, and my beloved is mine

אֱמוּנָה בַּטָחוֹן

Faith

אם אני לא עצמי, מי אני אהיה

If I am not myself, who will I be?

THE CYRILLIC/RUSSIAN ALPHABET

Aspects of the Cyrillic alphabet are used by a host of languages in Eastern Europe, principally Russian, but also Serbian, Bulgarian, Ukrainian and Macedonian, to name a few. Some Asian countries also employ the Cyrillic letter system – Kazakhstan, Uzbekistan, Kyrgyzstan and Mongolia – perhaps because it's a whole lot easier to learn than Arabic or Chinese.

Beginning with the letter 'A' and ending with 'Я', the 33 characters of the Cyrillic alphabet comprise an almost perfectly phonetic language, which makes for easy translation into English, although it's not so easy going the other way – tattoo artists beware! Many letters are similar to their counterparts in the Latin alphabet, with six that perform identically.

Мой разум не колодец, он никогда не иссякнет

My mind is not a well, it will not run dry

А Б В Г Д Е Ё Ж З

И Й К Л М Н О П Р С Т У

Ф Х Ц Ч Ш Щ Ъ Ы Ь Э Ю Я

а б в г д е ё ж з

и й к л м н о п р с т у

ф х ц ч ш щ ъ ы ь э ю я

Тяжело в ученье, легко в бою

Hard learning pays later
(Russian proverb)

Меня ничем не остановишь

There is nowhere I stop and you begin

CYRILLIC'S HISTORY

The story of the Cyrillic alphabet begins in the ninth century CE with the Greek monk, Saint Cyril. Accompanied by his brother, Saint Methodius, Cyril was dispatched on a mission to the Balkans to make Christians out of a tribe of Slavs. Cyril's job was to concoct an alphabet for standard use in Slavic churches. His raw materials were a curious mix of Greek, Hebrew and old Latin. Basing his writing system on his native Greek, Cyril invented a highly artistic alphabet called the 'Glagolitic' alphabet, after glagol, the fourth letter of his new alphabet, which may have come from Old Slavic, meaning 'to speak.' While Cyril's alphabet was winning Vatican approval, one of Cyril's students, under the direction of Tsar Simeon of Bulgaria, was working on an alphabet that would enable the writing of the Old Church Slavonic language. It was this alphabet that, for reasons not clear, immortalised Saint Cyril.

Based on the Greek capital letters, Cyrillic found its special personality with the addition of a handful of new letters to accommodate uniquely Slavic sounds. For the next few hundred years, Cyrillic was widely used in the Eastern European countries that had adopted Christianity, including Russia. Early evidence of Cyrillic script dates back to tenth-century Bulgaria, eleventh-century Russia and twelfth-century Bosnia and Serbia. Over time, the alphabet experienced the usual growing pains, before giving way to the popularity of the Latin letters, until today the only language that preserves Cyrillic in its original form is Old Church Slavic, which serves the Orthodox religion in Eastern Europe.

Russia developed more relaxed cursive forms of the alphabet over time and, in 1708, Peter the Great oversaw the Europeanisation of Cyrillic by removing its Greek flavour wherever possible. Upper- and lowercase letters were introduced, with capitals assigned the job of starting a sentence. At the same time, the Russian language imported words from German, French, even English. With the Russian Revolution (1918), the alphabet underwent a further cleansing. Exotic, non-phonetic letters were dropped, leaving the Cyrillic alphabet where it stands today, a phonetic writing system in which almost all words are spelt as they sound. To make things even easier for speakers of most Western languages, Cyrillic has 'Latinized' its look, adopting modern Latin fonts for both print and computer media.

PRISON CULTURE

While Cyrillic tattoos haven't exactly become a fashion trend in the West, there is a nexus of indelible Cyrillic body art in Russia's populous prisons. The British spy TV series *Spooks* featured Richard Armitage playing an agent who had just emerged from an eight-year spell in a Russian jail. He's covered in text tattoos, including one down his arm that translates as, 'See nothing, hear nothing, and say nothing to anybody'.

Свобода

Freedom

Февраль. Достать чернил и плакать,
Писать о феврале навзрыд,
Пока грохочущая слякоть
Весною черною горит.

Above: The first stanza from Black Spring
by Russian poet Boris Leonidovich
Pasternak

Black spring! Pick up your
pen, and weeping,
Of February, in sobs and ink,
Write poems, while the slush in thunder
Is burning in the black of spring.

(Translation by Lydia Pasternak Slater)

CHINESE CHARACTERS

A Chinese character is a logogram, meaning a sign that represents a word. A reported 50,000 of these characters make up the writing system for the Chinese language. That number has been officially slashed to a more manageable 6,000.

Arguably the oldest surviving writing system in the world, the Chinese characters, also known as 'hanzi' characters, are said to have been invented by an official in the court of the legendary Emperor Huangdi in 2600 BCE. Cangjie was his name, and he must have been indefatigable to invent such a vast number of pictograms. Most likely he collected and collated characters that were scattered throughout ancient China, and may have begun to standardise these proto-writings in order to turn them into a true writing system, the first evidence of which are inscriptions found on bone and tortoiseshell dating back to the Shang Dynasty (1766–1123 BCE). Thousands of years later, modern Chinese characters still bear a resemblance to the script on those famous 'oracle bones'.

勇氣

courage

幸福

happiness

尊重

respect

武

warrior

力

power

愛

love

和諧

harmony

賢

wisdom

自由

freedom

PICTO-PHONETIC CHARACTERS

Among those first characters were depictions of common objects, such as a tree and moon, a hand and foot, a mountain and sun. These simple characters were combined to form little 'stories', or affixed with an 'indicator' to form more complex characters that served to denote abstract concepts. The symbols morphed slowly over time, so that nowadays a good imagination is required to recognise the original object.

This category of character now makes up a tiny fraction of the Chinese writing system, and today most of the characters – 90 per cent of them – are picto-phonetic compounds, meaning that they're used for their sounds instead of their meaning. The English equivalent would be drawing an eye to portray 'I', waves to mean 'see', and the letter 'U' for 'you' ('I see you'). In this way, Chinese is really a means to represent the spoken language.

Written in columns, the Chinese characters are read from top to bottom, and from right to left.

MANDARIN AND CANTONESE

Although Mandarin and Cantonese are two distinct languages, the writing system for each is the same. Pronunciation may prevent these languages from being mutually intelligible.

雄英

hero

活生

live

神精

spirit

平和

peace

貴珍

precious

JAPANESE KANJI

Japan embraced literacy in the fourth century CE, when the Japanese borrowed pictograms from the Chinese and the Koreans, a system of characters called 'hanzi'. The Japanese called them 'kanji', meaning 'Han characters', and they survive to this day as part of the Japanese writing system.

Although the Japanese adopted the Chinese characters, the Chinese language was entirely alien to them. In fact, the Chinese and Japanese languages are from completely different linguistic families. The Japanese were forced to creatively reconfigure the characters to fit their own tongue. They used them phonetically and as logograms to convey an object or idea. The Japanese also incorporated two more 'alphabets' called 'katakana' and 'hiragana', each with their own function. Reading Japanese therefore requires the ability to negotiate between three distinct writing systems.

竜

dragon

力

strength

遠永

eternity

虎

tiger

天

the heavens

心安

tranquility

和平

peace

敬

respect

神

spirit

幸

happiness

COMPLICATIONS

The Japanese kanji logograms, like the Egyptian hieroglyphs, convey ideas in a pictorial form. They provide the root and core meaning of most nouns, adjectives and verbs. Hiragana symbols are often added after kanji as grammatical modifiers. For example, the Japanese kanji character for 'eat' could be modified to mean 'to eat', 'ate' or 'eating' by changing the hiragana characters that follow. But what makes kanji especially difficult to learn is the sheer number of symbols. Japanese schoolchildren must learn a basic vocabulary of 1,000 characters by the sixth grade. Almost 2,000 kanji are in everyday use, and about 3,500 characters are at the disposal of the well-educated Japanese person. Once you're versed in the vocabulary, there's the concept of context to consider, since where each character finds itself can alter its pronunciation.

KANJI TATTOOS

Kanji tattoos account for nearly 20 per cent of all Internet tattoo design searches. The idea of expressing a soulful feeling with such an exotic symbol is highly attractive. And the pitfalls are legendary. For starters, kanji is not a traditional Japanese tattoo. It's virtually unknown in Japan. But it's a tattoo style that has become popular among Westerners who believe that kanji identifies them with an Eastern culture based on geishas and cherry blossom. However, as a foreign writing system, kanji is a minefield lying in wait for the unsuspecting Westerner. Lyle Tuttle, arguably one of the most important tattooists in the modern history of tattooing, has long rejected requests to do kanji. He doesn't trust what he doesn't know, and what might take a lifetime to master.

Built not on alphabetical letters but on pictographs consisting of up to 30 strokes of the calligrapher's pen, kanji is a complex system in which each character can potentially entertain more than one 'reading'. Determining which of its possible meanings applies requires enough linguistic knowledge to accurately analyse the context. Some kanji can have up to 10 interpretations.

KANJI SCRIPT

Shodo is the Japanese term for calligraphy, or 'way of writing'. Kaisho is the angular block script commonly used for Japanese kanji tattoos, but never in everyday use. However, kanji may be written in the less legible script called sosho (cursive) or gyosho (semi-cursive), depending on how loose and flowing the client feels is right for him- or herself. After all, choosing a text style is always a reflection of personality, no less than choosing the thought the kanji conveys. In fact, some shodo masters insist that you don't necessarily have to know the meaning of a written symbol, since what matters most in calligraphy is the line and rhythm, which are reflections of the state of mind. You might say that the wearer of a text tattoo is literally 'writing their heart on their sleeve'.

HAIKU TATTOOS

Haiku tattoos have taken kanji to new heights of popularity. A haiku is a poem consisting of only a few syllables that capture the moment. For example: 'A world of grief and pain. Flowers bloom. Even then'. Take Lyle Tuttle's advice and find a native speaker of Japanese to design your haiku, because bad kanji can take you to new depths of humiliation.

harmony

wisdom

freedom

SEE FOR YOURSELF
If you don't speak Japanese, how do you know for certain that your choice of kanji says what you intend, and isn't going to be the source of eternal embarrassment? Visit Hanzi Smatter, a website entirely dedicated to the misuse of kanji characters in Western culture.

THE ELVISH ALPHABET

A tattoo design using the Elvish alphabet symbolises a belief in the magical, the power of imagination and fantasy and a desire to aspire to all the best qualities embodied by the Elven race.

Elvish is the language spoken by the race of Elves in *The Lord of the Rings*, and the nine main cast members of the popular movie trilogy all got tattoos in Elvish as a memento of their time spent on the picture. It is a testament to the breadth of JRR Tolkien's vision and imagination that the Elvish alphabet or script should be such a popular tattoo motive.

Tolkien is today best known as the author of *The Hobbit* and *The Lord of the Rings* trilogy. The success of those novels spawned an entire genre of fantasy fiction, of invented worlds and realms. Tolkien's passion for language and literature, and his gift for linguistics, were the genesis for his creation of Elvish and other languages. Tolkien himself asserted that much of his writing grew out of the languages he created and the mythologies he constructed around them.

warrior

happiness

love

courage

harmony

freedom

THE ELVEN LANGUAGE

Tolkien's Elves are reminiscent of those featured in many Scandinavian and Northern European myths and stories. Elves have special, even magical gifts, and they are often featured in the tales of humans who are on a quest or journey of self-discovery. The Elvish language

that Tolkien created drew heavily from Finnish and Welsh.

The popularity of Tolkien's writings has created an international following of scholars, enthusiasts and hobbyists who are devoted to the study of his invented languages, of which Elvish is the primary focus.

musical notations

'Music produces a kind of pleasure which human nature cannot do without', said Confucius, the ancient Chinese philosopher.

The very sight of musical symbols is enough to put some people in that pleasurable mood of which he spoke, which perhaps explains why people incorporate musical motifs within their tattoo designs. The most recognisable signs in the musical realm are the treble clef, the staff and the notes.

CLEF

Clef is French for 'key', and it is the first sign we encounter on a sheet of music. It is superimposed over the five lines of the staff, and its purpose is to indicate the pitch of the written notes. The familiar treble clef looks like a grandiose 'S', but its critical component is the curl. The line on the staff that passes through that curl is identified as G, which is why it's also called the G-clef. By identifying G, the other notes on the staff – E, B, D, F – are also known, since their relationship to G never changes. Similarly, the F-clef, also called the bass clef, assigns the note F to the line on the staff that falls between the two dots of the clef.

The treble clef can be seen as either a stylized 'G' or 'S', and there is a connection between the two. The syllable 'sol' was the name given to G in the medieval system for naming notes, which is still in use today – do, re, me, fa, so, la, ti, do. Those syllables were drawn from the first syllables of each successive verse in a choral hymn to Saint John the Baptist, around CE 1000. At some point in its evolution, 'sol' was shortened to 'so', so that all the syllables ended in a vowel.

MUSICAL NOTES

The musical note has three distinct parts. The rounded head is either white (open), or black (closed). Other than whole notes (or double whole notes), the note sign comes with a stem and a flag to indicate its (shorter) time value.

Historically, all notes started out as solid black, but with the introduction of paper in Europe, scribes struggled to keep the ink from bleeding along the fibres and creating a blob. The solution was to use less ink, and the best way to do that was to draw notes in outline. With that, the white note was born.

ANCIENT MUSICAL SYSTEMS

Cultures much more ancient than the Europeans had devised systems for denoting music, including the Egyptians, the Chinese and early peoples living in Anatolia (modern Turkey). As early as 200 BCE the Greeks applied a system of 'accents' to texts that were meant to be sung. The oldest evidence of a complete musical composition from Western cultures is the Greek Seikilos Epitaph.

MONOGRAMS

Monograms are an artistic rendering of an individual's initials, or a skilful combination of more than one person's initials.

These 'signatures' go back centuries, and today they're found everywhere from personal stationery to the leather seats of luxury cars. Most commonly, monograms are found on towels, handbags and luggage, and more recently inked on human skin as tattoos.

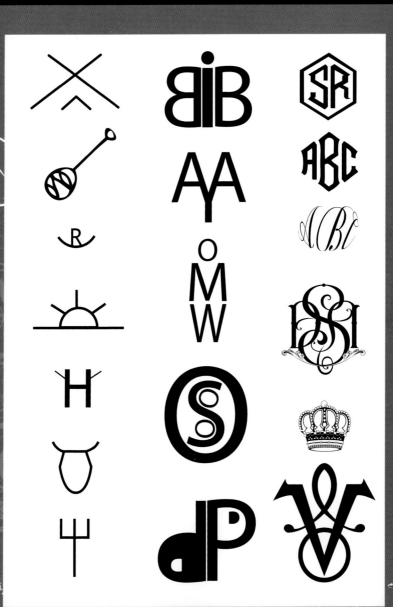

HISTORICAL MONOGRAMS

Monograms probably first appeared on the earliest currency: clay coins imprinted with the initials of the local king. Ancient Greeks and Romans certainly adopted that convention. This abbreviated royal signature soon appeared on other precious royal objects, especially those made of gold and silver, but also on weapons, banners and coats of arms. Even today, a monarch's initials may appear on the insignia of a country's public agencies.

A coin with a monogram of Peter the Great from the early eighteenth century

Jesus had his own monogram, posthumously of course, which dates back to the first century. 'Ihs' derives from the Greek letters iota, eta and sigma, which are the first three letters in the Greek word for 'Jesus'. As an abbreviation, convention required the addition of a horizontal bar over the letters.

Coins from the reign of Charlemagne (late eighth century CE) feature a monogram that doubled as the emperor's signature, since he was illiterate. To authorize documents, Charlemagne had a scribe draw the four letters, 'KRLS', after which 'Charles the Bald' would link them with his own pen and ink.

By the Middle Ages, artisans recognised the value of the monogram as a way to mark the authenticity of their furniture and artworks, and by Victorian times the monogram gained more widespread use as a symbol that advertised an aristocrat's place in society. While single-initial monograms and two-letter monograms may have once prevailed, the three-letter monogram had become the standard.

PROTOCOL

Traditional monogram design was restricted by etiquette. The rules were few and simple. For the female monogram, they dictated that the first initial be positioned on the left, the middle initial on the right and the family initial in the middle, but larger. A male convention developed that kept all letters the same size, which required them to be arranged in their natural order. For the married woman, her initials would line up as first name, maiden name, married name (unless retaining her maiden name).

Name combinations arising from marriage can get complicated, but usually consist of the bride's first initial on the left, the groom's first initial on the right and the shared family initial larger in the centre. Double-barrelled names pose a special challenge, leaving designers to remember that the foremost rule is simplicity: although a monogram does include a set of letters, the whole idea is to create a graphic character that is immediately perceived as a unified design.

The rules for monogram tattoos are still in the making, but some would warn against monograms for people who aren't legally married. And if they are hitched, 'avoid hyphens', some would caution. Others insist that the hyphen signifies a degree of mutual independence in the relationship, and is therefore necessary. Otherwise, stick to three letters for maximum graphic appeal.

TALISMANIC MONOGRAMS

As well as monograms in the Latin alphabet, there is a tradition in existence of runic monograms, called 'bindrunes', used as talismans. Up to five runes may be arranged to create a harmonious design. A single rune often serves as the central character, upon which the other runes are added to reinforce the power or intention. Always bear in mind, however, that overlapping such angular symbols might accidentally create other runic shapes.

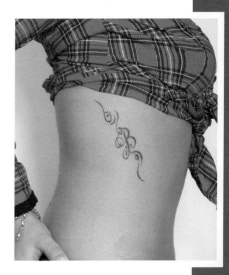

You could achieve a monogram using Ornament fonts surrounding a single letter, as here, the letter B

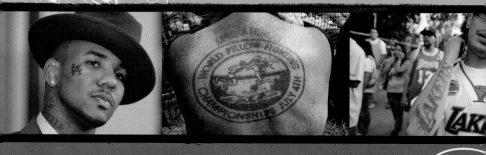

LOGOS

Taking on a corporate logo tattoo may look for all the world like a celebration of mass conformity, but is that the case? Are logo tattoos a symptom of our collective addiction to the buzz words and brand names of our consumer culture? Or, are they some kind of ironic postmodern challenge to that very idea? Perhaps, at the very least, these Madison Avenue hieroglyphs are a form of pop art.

Logo tattoos took off in the 1990s when certain restaurants offered a 'free lunch forever' in exchange for anyone who would ink the restaurant name on their body. More recently, the online gambling site, Goldenpalace.com, offered a woman $10,000 to tattoo their domain name on her forehead. She did it – to put her child through school.

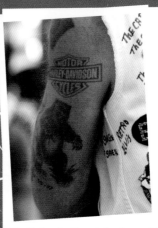

The Harley Davidson tattoo is one of the most popular logo tattoos around

INCLUSIVITY OF LOGOS

There doesn't appear to be anything individualistic about wearing a corporate logo tattoo, yet 'expressing my individuality' and 'claiming ownership of my body' remain popular reasons for taking on any tattoo. The best logo tattoos may still do that, performing the all-important task of connecting us with necessarily invisible aspects of our deeper selves.

Like gang tattoos, the corporate logo tattoo marks the owner as a member of a unique group. Whatever one's bias towards 'the corporation', there's an undeniable human proclivity to belong to a community of like-minded people.

Indigenous tribes around the world have traditionally employed the tattoo for just that reason. Within the group, the tattoo is about conforming, about marking rites of passage and generally about surrendering one's personal likes and dislikes for the advancement of the common good. Outside the group is another matter. Among strangers, the tattoo sets the person apart.

Consider the Harley Davidson tribe. Harley Davidson tattoos are believed to be America's most popular logo tattoo (although Nike might have a word or three – 'Just do it' – to say about that). Do people commission the clean bold caps of 'Harley Davidson' out of a sense of brand loyalty, or is there a tribal factor at work here?

The company's corporate strategy is unabashedly based on 'the tribe', featuring a division with the sole responsibility of nurturing their faithful community. On the company's recent 105th anniversary ride, the company president made it clear that he wasn't participating as CEO, but simply as a member of 'the tribe that rides.'

A theory of logo infatuation suggests that everything in society, including the human body, has become commodified. The body is a 'prisoner of the culture', said French social critic, Michel Foucault. Has life in the West reached the point where brands are so enslaving us that they now serve as the objects of our fetishistic obsessions? Not the product, by the way, but the brand. Or, more accurately, the brand image, which is a kind of mirage. We know that corporate psychologists have been working long and hard to ensure that their pseudo-philosophies become the objects of our identification, so, should we be questioning our logo-motives? If it's true that we're not really interested in helping corporations sell more shoes or gasoline, what are logo tattoos actually expressing? Corporate answer: a lifestyle. If you buy a Jeep, you're buying a million square miles of American off-road adventure – in your dreams. And what are tattoos but the outward reflection of our inner landscapes?

The world now glitters incessantly amidst a perpetual festival of advertising signs and slogans. Living in a consumer society with all its freedoms and wealth, we've almost lost interest in the object of most advertising, and instead we consume the virtual reality that radiates from every overblown ad campaign. The message may be meaningless, but if we nevertheless find it appealing, we upload it into our virtual hopes and aspirations.

The crown logo, itself a symbol of royalty, has been used for many other purposes, including a Vivienne Westwood fashion campaign

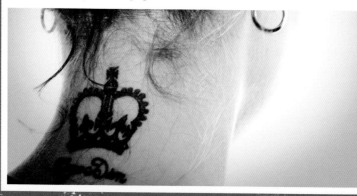

Some logos have themselves become a fashion statement. Above: The Chanel logo is perfect for the ultimate fashionista. Below: The Converse trainer logo is also a fun alternative

It is worth remembering that some designs carry a tremendous amount of baggage with them. Logos can cause problems if some kind of controversy or company disaster occurs. Designs that are used as symbols by gangs or extremist groups, or that are associated with hate crimes, are almost certainly ones you should avoid. Most reputable tattoo artists, for example, would never dream of tattooing a swastika on a client. Tattoos of profanity, that are sexually explicit or that might be racially offensive, will probably cause no end of grief when it comes time to get a job, and in some circumstances certain tattoo designs will make finding employment exceedingly difficult.

AMBIGRAMS

An increasingly popular motif in tattoo parlours is the ambigram, a graphic figure that can be flipped, mirrored or inverted, yet whichever way it is viewed still spells out the same thing. The shifting positive and negative spaces play tricks on our visual perception, casting a spell on the beholder.

Sometimes referred to as an 'inversion' or 'flipscript', for tattoo aficionados a whole dictionary of ambigram designs is available, and a great range of scripts and fonts, from simply elegant to graphically Gothic. A design may consist of a single word or an entire phrase. Depending on the ambigram's concept, it can be rotated, reversed or reflected in mirrors, with the meaning sometimes remaining the same, sometimes changing: looked at one way, you might see 'devil', but turn it around and 'angel' appears. The best tattoo artists can create an optical illusion with a graphic design that never fails to intrigue.

Ambigrams are exercises in graphic design that play with optical illusions, symmetry and visual perception. Many people choose to get an ambigram tattoo on their forearm, where they can flip it one way or the other, giving viewers the full effect of the design.

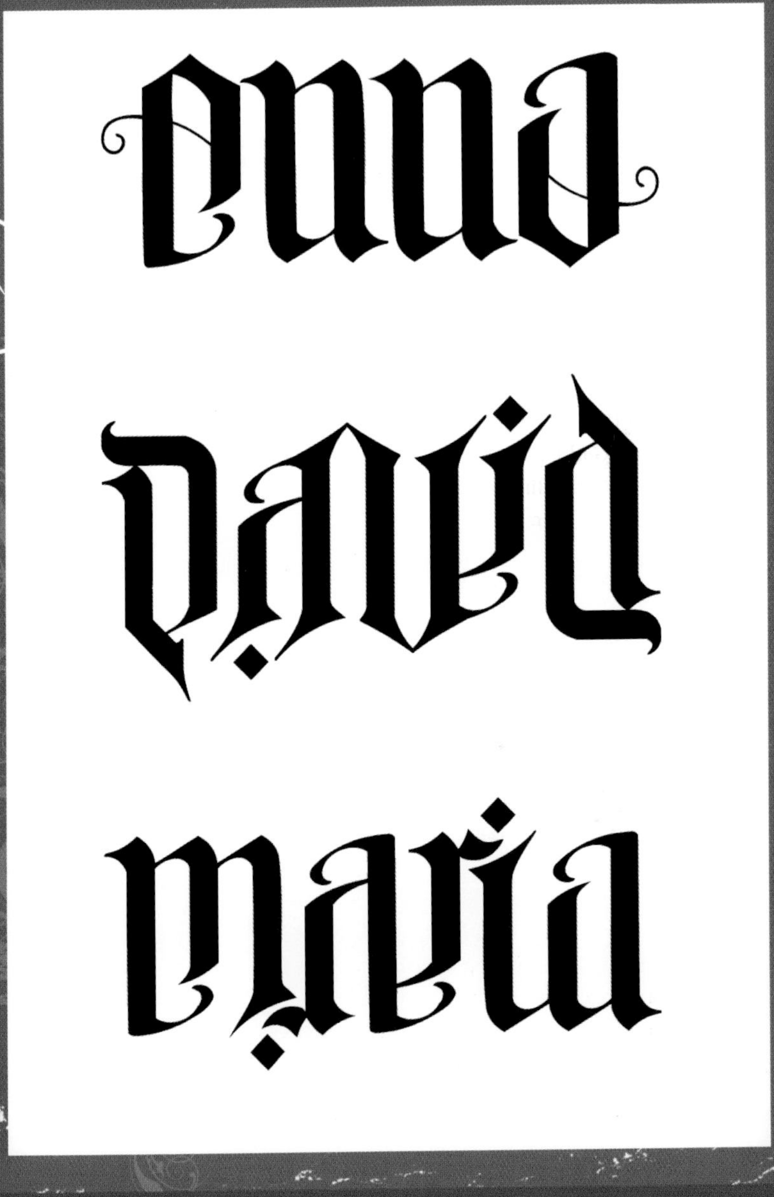
anna
david
maria

GAINING POPULARITY

According to practitioner John Langdon, ambigrams were independently invented by himself and Scott Kim in the 1970s. Kim used the name 'Inversions' as the title for his first collection in 1981. The first published reference to ambigrams was by Douglas Hofstadter, who attributes the origin of the word to conversations among a small group of friends from 1983 to 1984. The 1999 edition of Hofstadter's *Gödel, Escher, Bach* features a three-dimensional ambigram on the cover.

John Langdon is truly one of the great ambigramists, his work appearing on the covers of some recent bestselling books. The popularity of ambigrams soared when they were intertwined into the plot of Dan Brown's bestseller *Angels and Demons*. Langdon produced ambigrams that were used for the book cover, and a link to his website from Brown's meant he was 'suddenly inundated' with commissions. In fact, the name Robert Langdon (the novel's hero) is used in homage to John Langdon.

Toryn Green from the American band Fuel sports two ambigram tattoos – Angel/Devil and Sinner/Saint

CATEGORIES

ROTATIONAL

This design presents several instances of words when rotated through a fixed angle, usually 180 degrees, although rotational ambigrams of other angles exist, for example 90 or 45 degrees.

FIGURE-GROUND

With this design the spaces between the letters of one word form another word. The above is an Escher-style design which reads Allah in Arabic font.

SYMBIOTOGRAM

Any ambigram that, when rotated 180 degrees, can be read as a different word than the original. The above ambigram reads both 'Amore' (love in Italian) and 'Dolore' (pain in Italian).

CHAIN

In this instance a word (or sometimes words) is interlinked, forming a repeating chain. The above reads 'Memento Mori' in a circle-style chain ambigram.

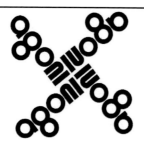

Fractal

A version of space-filling ambigrams, where the tiled word branches from itself and then shrinks in a self-similar manner, forming a fractal. The above example reads 'agonie' (agony in Italian) from four different angles.

Perceptual shift

This design has no symmetry but can be read as two different words depending on how the curves of the letters are interpreted. The above example can read both 'I love you!' and 'Hate you!' depending on how you read the letters.

Natural

Mirror

A natural ambigram possesses one or more of the above symmetries when written in its natural state, requiring no typographic styling. For example, the words 'dollop' and 'suns' are natural rotational ambigrams. The word 'bud' forms a natural mirror ambigram when reflected over a vertical axis. The words 'CHOICE' and 'OXIDE', all in capitals, form a natural mirror ambigram when reflected over a horizontal axis. The word 'TOOTH' all in capitals forms a natural mirror ambigram when its letters are stacked vertically and reflected over a vertical axis. The example 'Mom', above, is a great idea for a natural ambigram.

This design can be read in a mirror, usually as the same word or phrase both ways. Ambigrams that form different words when viewed in the mirror are also known as 'glass door' ambigrams, because they can be printed on a glass door to be read differently when entering or exiting. This design 'Love & Hate' and 'War and Peace' would be a great design for a tattoo – and personal as it is you yourself who would see the reflected phrase in the mirror.

SCROLLS, BANNERS & RIBBONS

Text tattoos can sometimes seem lost on an expanse of skin, so tattoo artists use scrolls to display text, either on its own or as a specific design element within a larger motif.

You don't have to look far for examples. Hearts and roses are two tattoo designs that routinely come with a blank banner waiting to be filled in with the appropriate text. Memorial tattoos that feature a wide array of cherubs, angels and other religious symbols often come with banners that can be used to give information regarding who is being remembered, or a place for appropriate dates. Military and patriotic tattoos not only come with banners, but more often than not they also come with the text and letters supplied, 'Army', 'Navy', 'Air Force', 'Marines', 'Death Before Dishonour', 'A Sailor's Grave' and 'Homeward Bound'. The list goes on.

AESTHETICALLY PLEASING

The artful use of scrolls, ribbons and banners not only allows the tattoo artist to use text in an aesthetically pleasing way, but also to integrate the tattoo design with other body art in a harmonious fashion. Ribbons and banners can also be wrapped around arms, wrists and ankles, and draped over shoulders and around waists. The tattoo artist and the client are limited in their use only by their imaginations.

text tattoos on the fingers

The poetry and pain, beauty and angst that can be contained in a mere eight letters of the alphabet is nothing short of inspiring. In eight letters, one on each finger, you can express the human condition better than many novels and most Hollywood movies, although it must be said that, on occasion, spelling, grammar and syntax are taken on a leap of faith.

For the better part of the last century, hand tattoos, more specifically text tattoos inked on the tops of the fingers, often better known as 'knuckledusters', were perhaps the defining demarcation line between the tattoo enthusiasts and aficionados and the truly hardcore. And to be hardcore meant not giving a damn about whether or not the world knew you were tattooed, and caring even less about what said world thought about your tattoos.

POPULAR KNUCKLEDUSTERS

Hand tattoos have their roots in the working-class traditions and superstitions of sailors and a life at sea. Over time they have evolved to become a particularly powerful way to declare one's politics, philosophy and personal view of the world.

LOVE HATE	**LOVE AND HATE** Made famous in the film noir classic, *Night of the Hunter*, where it was worn on the hands of preacher Harry Powell, played by Robert Mitchum.
ROCK ROLL	**ROCK & ROLL** If you're going to be a rock star, it pays to brand yourself.

FAVOURITE WORDS TO LIVE & LOVE BY

The following popular words for tattoos have been culled from more than a dozen different languages and many cultures from all over the globe. These words can be loosely grouped into the following categories, and they often overlap. Where does family begin and love end, for example? It will come as no surprise that the most popular text tattoos are 'Love', 'Family' and 'Friendship'. And the most popular virtue and motto for living is 'Strength', in all its many permutations.

FAMILY TIES

GRANDFATHER

Grandfather

Father

Father

MOTHER

Mother

Sister

Sister

BROTHER

Brother

SON

Son

Daughter

Daughter

Beloved

Beloved

Grandmother

Grandmother

Blood

Blood

WAY OF LİFE

EXTREME

Extreme

Jezebel

Jezebel

CHOICE

Choice

Legend

Legend

CONQUER

Conquer

Ninja

Ninja

HARDCORE

Hardcore

Outsider

Outsider

WAY OF LİFE conт...

Rogue

Vigilante

Lady

Artist

Outlaw

Shaman

Rocker

Saint

WAY OF LİFE cont...

Rasta

Rasta

PIRATE

Pirate

Witch

Witch

WARRIOR

Warrior

Sailor

Sailor

ΠΑΤVRE

Paradise

Paradise

Wave

Wave

Mountain

Mountain

water

Water

Sun

Sun

ΠΑΤ∪RE cont...

River

River

THUNDER

Thunder

ROCK

Rock

Chrysalis

Chrysalis

Sky

Sky

𝔑𝔦𝔤𝔥𝔱

Night

Wind

Wind

Rose

Rose

LOVE & ANGUISH

AGONY

Agony

Lost

Lost

DEATH

Death

Inferno

Inferno

CHAOS

Chaos

Tears

Tears

Grief

Grief

JUSTICE

Justice

LOVE & ANGUISH cont...

Heartache

Heartache

Struggle

Struggle

Never

Never

PAIN

Pain

regret

Regret

LOVE & CHERISH

Love

Love

Always

Always

Adore

Adore

Cherish

Cherish

Beauty

Beauty

Sensual

Sensual

awe

Awe

Bliss

Bliss

LOVE & CHERISH cont...

Feminine

Feminine

MASCULINE

Masculine

Believe

Believe

𝔉𝔬𝔯𝔢𝔳𝔢𝔯

Forever

Perfect

Perfect

Diamond

Diamond

BRIGHT

Bright

ecstasy

Ecstasy

LOVE & CHERISH cont...

Delicious

Delicious

Flirt

Flirt

Kiss

Kiss

HOT

Hot

Foxy

Foxy

Juicy

Juicy

cherry

Cherry

SUGAR

Sugar

LOVE & CHERiSH cont...

voluptuous

Voluptuous

gift

Gift

Sensual

Sensual

CHANCE

Chance

Romantic

Romantic

SWEET

Sweet

Serene

Serene

DIAMOND

Diamond

LİVİΠG LİFE

imagine

Imagine

𝕭alance

Balance

destiny

Destiny

heal

Heal

Wonder

Wonder

LİVİNG LİFE cont...

Recovery
Recovery

light
Light

LIFE
Life

JOURNEY
Journey

Dream
Dream

free
Free

Freedom
Freedom

FORGET
Forget

LİVİΠG LİFE conт...

remember

Remember

HOPE

Hope

Quest

Quest

happiness

Happiness

LIBERTINE

Libertine

incandescent

Incandescent

Friendship

Friendship

Endless

Endless

VIRTUES

Understanding

Understanding

Fortitude

Fortitude

INTREPID

Intrepid

Bravery

Bravery

COURAGE

Courage

Endurance

Endurance

Dauntless

Dauntless

ViRTUES cont...

Fierce

Notorious

Notorious

HONOUR

Honour

PATRIOT

Patriot

Diligence

Diligence

`fame`

Fame

Noble

Noble

Chastity

Chastity

VIRTUES cont...

Perseverance

Perseverance

HERO

Hero

Loyalty

Loyalty

Generosity

Generosity

LEADER

Leader

GENIUS

Genius

inspire

Inspire

Good

Good

VIRTUES cont...

MERCY

Mercy

Innocence

Innocence

Forgiveness

Forgiveness

Patience

Patience

FIDELITY

Fidelity

Compassion

Compassion

humility

Humility

Gentle

Gentle

VIRTUES cont...

EQUALITY

Equality

Purity

Purity

pleasure

Pleasure

Luscious

Luscious

Luminous

Luminous

PROTECTION

Protection

Decadent

Decadent

Passion

Passion

ViRTUES cont...

REBEL	OVERCOME
Rebel	Overcome
Lucky	SPEED
Lucky	Speed
RELIANT	Perfection
Reliant	Perfection
knowledge	STAMINA
Knowledge	Stamina

VİCES

ANARCHY

Anarchy

Lust

Lust

Heartless

Heartless

Desire

Desire

Envy

Envy

Naughty

Naughty

Erotic

Erotic

VICES cont...

Evil	POWER
Evil	Power
Mischievous	Hate
Mischievous	Hate
Gluttony	Guilty
Gluttony	Guilty
Greed	Wild
Greed	Wild

VİCES cont...

Ego

Wrath

Temptation

Kill

Rage

Scoundrel

Gambler

Sloth

RELIGIOUS & SPIRITUAL

God

God

divine

Divine

Disciple

Disciple

divinity

Divinity

BLESSED

Blessed

Spirit

Spirit

buddha

Buddha

infinity

Infinity

RELIGIOUS & SPIRITUAL cont...

eternity

Eternity

Heaven

Heaven

Faith

Faith

Pray

Pray

angel

Angel

Religious

Religious

reincarnation

Reincarnation

Goddess

Goddess

RELiGiOUS & SPiRiTUAL cont...

Grace

Grace

miracle

Miracle

SACRED

Sacred

ΩMEGA

Omega

HELL

Hell

ALPHA

Alpha

Dharma

Dharma

Reborn

Reborn

RELIGIOUS & SPIRITUAL cont...

Redemption

Redemption

Repent

Repent

DEVIL

Devil

Resurrection

Resurrection

Soul

Soul

SACRED

Sacred

Demon

Demon

Sacrifice

Sacrifice

cosmic

COMET

Comet

COSMIC

Cosmic

karma

Karma

Moon

Moon

Supernova

Supernova

Earth

Earth

Hedonist

Hedonist

cosmic

SHAPE-SHIFTER

Shape-shifter

Magic

Immortal

Immortal

druid

Druid

Infinity

Infinity

Harmony

Harmony

Eternity

Eternity

Mystic

GREEK ZODIAC

Capricorn

Cancer

Aquarius

Leo

Pisces

Virgo

Aries

Libra

Taurus

Scorpio

Gemini

Sagittarius

CHINESE ZODIAC

Rat

Horse

Ox

Sheep

Tiger

Monkey

Rabbit

Cockerel

Dragon

Dog

Snake

Pig

talismans, totems & amulets

EAGLE	SNAKE
Eagle	Snake
HAWK	CAT
Hawk	Cat
PHOENIX	*RAVEN*
Phoenix	Raven
UNICORN	WOLF
Unicorn	Wolf

TALISMANS, TOTEMS & AMULETS

Dragon

Dragon

Coyote

Coyote

Viper

Viper

Bear

Bear

Cobra

Cobra

RAT

Rat

Dog

Dog

Fox

Fox

talismans, totems & amulets

FIRE

Fire

Goat

Goat

SWORD

Sword

Bull

Bull

SHARK

Shark

SHIELD

Shield

Lion

Lion

Anchor

Anchor

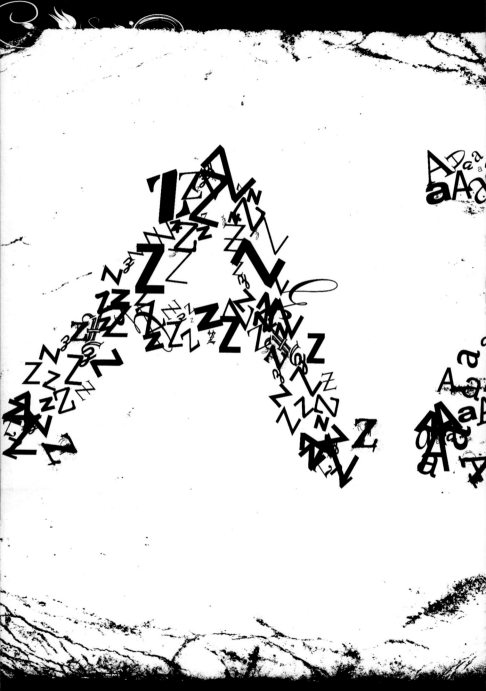

THE TATTOO FONT LIBRARY
A HISTORY OF TYPEFACES
AND FONTS GARALDE
SLAB SERIF HUMANIST
TRANSITIONAL GLYPHIC
BLACKLETTER CASUAL SCRIPT
FORMAL SCRIPT DECORATED/
ORNAMENTAL CALLIGRAPHIC
BEYOND CLASSIFICATION

A HISTORY OF TYPEFACES AND FONTS

Many people who choose to have a text tattoo, either on its own or as a key element in a larger design, will ask if they can see some tattoo fonts.

Depending on the design and genre of your proposed tattoo, and its placement on the body, different fonts may be better suited to different tattoos. Large Olde English lettering might be appropriate for the chest or broad back of a man, but would overwhelm the delicate wrist or ankle of a woman. A biblical or literary quotation may look best if it mimics the printed word, while a declaration of love may have greater emotional impact if the tattooed text appears to be written by hand. Other tattoos look as if they've been typed onto the skin with an old typewriter – shades of Ernest Hemingway and Raymond Chandler. The right choice of font can make all the difference in what a tattoo symbolises for its wearer. Before the modern era of tattooing, certain script styles were more common than others. Some of these typefaces drew their inspiration from the world in which the tattooist operated, the circus, for instance, where tattooed men and women were on display, and where tattoo artists did a booming business. The military had their own design motifs and corresponding fonts, as did the inhabitants of correctional institutions. Nobody discussed the typeface with the tattooist, who stuck to the few styles he knew best, lettering that the public came to recognize as 'tattoo fonts'.

BLACKLETTER

Fonts were born out of the printing business. Until the digital age, metal letters were made for repeated use in printing presses. The first fonts were cast in lead, such as that designed by the German Johannes Gutenberg to print his historic Bible in 1455. It was meant to resemble handwriting. Medieval scribes were masters of calligraphy, perfectionists at maintaining a consistency with each letter they drew. During the Roman Empire, inch-high Uncial lettering was the fashion, but that eventually gave way to an Irish Celtic Roundhand. King Charlemagne later standardised lettering by ordering a style called Carolingian to be used throughout the Holy Roman Empire. A penmanship style called Blackletter – also known as Olde English or Gothic – evolved in Germany. To print his famous Bible, Gutenberg adapted the Blackletter style in the making of his movable type. It was important that his printed books appeared to be hand-lettered, so they might successfully compete with the magnificent penwritten manuscripts. Gutenberg's Blackletter font was comprised of over 300 characters, including flourishes and ligatures (connecting flourishes), to replicate the hand-crafted Gothic script.

c.1483, The Nuremberg Chronicle, *Latin edition, displaying Gutenburg's font*

OLD STYLE & BEYOND

The modern history of type followed in the wake of Gutenberg. His whimsical Blackletter font was soon criticised for being too complex and difficult to read. Furthermore, its flourishes did not suit the mood of the Renaissance movement. The new humanism was more secular, practical and realistic. The age demanded a new font, something lighter, more legible and elegant and something that honoured classical Roman and Greek art. In fact, something that looked a lot like ancient Roman script itself. It was named Antiqua, later to become Old Style. Designed by Nicholas Jenson, a colleague of Gutenberg's, Old Style was characterised by 'diagonal stress', a ploy to replicate the leaning script of the early scribes. The thickness of strokes varied little, but the angled parts of the letters were generally the thinnest. This low-contrast font was hailed as extremely readable. With the proliferation of print shops in Europe, it wasn't long before other typefaces appeared, and so the art of typographic design was born. Many of the traditional fonts in use today in the West were designed before the early 1800s – including Times New Roman.

ROMAN AND ITALIC

The roman – or antique – style forms the basis of Western printed language. Our capital letters derive from the Latin monumental capitals (majuscules), circa CE 100, which were angular and upright. Carolingian minuscules (lowercase) from around CE 800 were a second inspiration for the roman style. Calligraphers used pen and ink on parchment to create these characters. Renaissance scribes later refined these two models to create the roman and italic fonts that have survived to the present day. Italic (meaning 'from Italy') typefaces became popular with printers because slanted words occupied less space on the page, allowing books to be smaller and therefore less expensive to produce, and because cursive fonts

with their connected characters were already a trend. These early italic fonts featured upright capitals with lowercase letters that were slanted to the right.

MODERN DAY

Typesetting today is largely a computer operation, and the computer age has spawned a font that couldn't be further from Gutenberg's highly flourished Olde English typeface. It's a humble, sans-serif font (lettering without any flares at the end of the stroke) called Arial. Microsoft felt that a sans-serif font would be more legible on a computer screen, so they licensed Arial as a cheaper alternative to the popular Helvetica. With the success of Windows and the personal computer, the Helvetica lookalike has become the digital standard.

POINTS

When describing fonts, we refer to their size in terms of 'points'. Type sizes have always been relative to the inch, which is divided into 72 points. The common 12-point font would therefore be one-sixth of an inch, also known as one 'pica'.

LIGATURES AND KERNING

It can be important for tattoo artists and those considering getting a text tattoo to familiarise themselves with some typographical terms. Ligatures are combinations of alphabet characters that have been designed as a single unit to create a harmonious and pleasant appearance. Historically, ligatures were carved as separate creations, and when the letter combinations in question appeared in the text to be printed, the appropriate ligature was put to good use. The best ligatures are works of art, the characters beautifully designed to work in unison.

fi fl ae oe   fi fl æ œ

plain text   *ligatures*

Kerning is the process of moving letters closer together or further apart so that they appear evenly spaced to the eye. This makes text easier to read on a page, but in a text tattoo, kerning is crucial from an aesthetic viewpoint. You will want the lettering in your text tattoo to appear balanced and properly

WAR
WAR
WAR

proportioned. Most fonts include kerning pairs (Ta, To, Tr, We, Wo, Po and so on) that adjust their spacing automatically when typed consecutively. In a tattoo, this will have to be done by the tattoo artist.

Tracking is a term used by software companies to describe manual kerning done by the software, as opposed to the hand kerning done by a typographer.

THE FONT LIBRARY

The classification of typefaces is a complex subject and continues to be a matter of debate among typographers and type historians.

The following directory is organised into eleven typeface families – a more simplified version than you would find in a typography book – so that you can begin looking at the way typefaces are formed and their context. The typefaces have been chosen for their popularity in tattoo design, and within each section are examples of fonts you could add to your portfolio.

You may find you like a typeface, and will be inspired to look at other fonts within it to find the perfect font for your chosen letters.

GARALDE

Garalde fonts (also known as Old Style or Old Face) include some of the most attractive and well-designed text faces. They are highly legible, but visually lively. Caslon is admired because of the harmony and consistency in how the letters fit together on the page – or indeed on the skin. It works well for longer, especially literary, quotes.

ADOBE CASLON

A B C D E F G H I J K L M
N O P Q R S T U V W X Y Z

a b c d e f g h i j k l m
n o p q r s t u v w x y z

a b c d e f g h i j k l m
n o p q r s t u v w x y z

0 1 2 3 4 5 6 7 8 9

. , & ! ? $ £ ß ƒ @ π μ ©

We are all in the gutter, but some of us are looking at the stars

Adobe Caslon Pro Regular

We are all in the gutter, but some of us are looking at the stars

Adobe Caslon Pro Bold

We are all in the gutter, but some of us are looking at the stars

Minion Italic

Minion Ornaments

THE PHRASE

This famous aspirational quote was first uttered by the writer Oscar Wilde.

WHAT IS AN ORNAMENT FONT?

In addition to the letters of the alphabet, digital fonts include a variety of non-alphabetical forms. Included in this are ornaments, which follow the style and feel of the typeface but offer an abstract face. These can work well as bands around the arm, or as additions to a phrase or word.

SLAB SERİF

At their best, Slab Serifs are both robust and colourful. They have a retro feel about them, because they were widely used in the 1950s and 1960s for advertising and design. They seem to work best in the heavier, bolder styles. Other fonts that would work well on skin from this typeface are Scala, and the bolder Aachen.

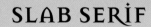

AMERICAN TYPEWRITER

A B C D E F G H I J K L M
N O P Q R S T U V W X Y Z

a b c d e f g h i j k l m
n o p q r s t u v w x y z

0 1 2 3 4 5 6 7 8 9

. , & ! ? $ £ ß ƒ @ π µ ©

Only God can judge me

American Typewriter Regular

Only God can judge me

American Typewriter Bold

Only God can judge me

Clarendon Light

Only God can judge me

Clarendon Roman

Only God can judge me

Clarendon Bold

THE PHRASE

'Only God can judge me' has two popular elements of text tattoos – both a religious connotation and an uplifting sentiment.

HVMANIST

Humanist typefaces, dating from the fifteenth century, represent the first major stylistic development in type design. They have considerable character and leave a classic impact – however, the irregularity of outline and small counters mean that they are not particularly legible at small sizes.

CENTAVR ROMAN

A B C D E F G H I J K L M
N O P Q R S T U V W X Y Z

a b c d e f g h i j k l m
n o p q r s t u v w x y z

0 1 2 3 4 5 6 7 8 9

. , & ! ? $ £ ß f @ µ ©

Fear ends where faith begins

Centaur Roman

Fear Ends Where Faith Begins

Centaur Swash MT

Blut ist dicker als Wasser

Garamond

Blut ist dicker als Wasser

Garamond Italic

Blut is dicker als Wasser

Garamond Bold

THE PHRASES

Faith and spirituality are a common theme for tattoos.

Blut ist dicker als Wasser: Blood is thicker than water (german)

WHAT IS A SWASH?

Some typefaces include fonts of swash characters, like the centaur swash above – this uses swash characters at the beginning of each word. These letters have greater decorative extravagance. Typefaces which are derived from calligraphic forms work well. A swash font may include alternate lowercase letters and other variant forms, such as ornaments (see page 161).

Transitional

Transitionals are, as a general rule, well suited to large bodies of text – although they can benefit from a fairly loose letter spacing or tracking. Baskerville is another font within this group which has very pleasing letterforms.

Stone Serif

A B C D E F G H I J K L M N
O P Q R S T U V W X Y Z

a b c d e f g h i j k l m
n o p q r s t u v w x y z

0 1 2 3 4 5 6 7 8 9

. , & ! ? $ £ ß *f* @ μ ©

The man who has no imagination has no wings

Stone Serif Medium

The man who has no imagination has no wings

Stone Serif Italic

Where there is love, there is life

Century Schoolbook Medium

Where there is love, there is life

Century Schoolbook Bold Italic

THE PHRASES

'THE MAN WHO HAS NO IMAGINATION HAS NO WINGS' IS ATTRIBUTED TO THE AMERICAN BOXER AND ACTIVIST MUHAMMED ALI.

'WHERE THERE IS LOVE, THERE IS LIFE' IS A QUOTE FROM MAHATMA GANDHI, INDIAN POLITICAL AND SPIRITUAL HERO.

GLYPHIC

Glyphics work well with Latin text because of their carved or inscribed type style. They are primarily a tilting form and many have no lowercase. Rusticana, Augustea Open and Sophia are other fonts within the Glyphic typeface which offer wonderfully sharp and graphic shapes for a short word with high visual impact.

LITHOS REGULAR

A B C D E F G H I J K L M
N O P Q R S T U V W X Y Z

A B C D E F G H I J K L M
N O P Q R S T U V W X Y Z

0 1 2 3 4 5 6 7 8 9

. , & ! ? $ £ SS f @ Π μ ©

PER ASPERA AD ASTRA

Lithos Regular

PER ASPERA AD ASTRA

Lithos Black

OMNIA VINCIT AMOR

Trajan Regular

OMNIA VINCIT AMOR

Trajan Bold

THE PHRASES

PER ASPERA AD ASTRA: THROUGH ADVERSITY TO THE STARS (LATIN).

OMNIA VINCIT AMOR: LOVE CONQUERS ALL (LATIN).

BLACKLETTER

Blackletter is one of the most popular fonts for tattoos. Although Daniel Will-Harris, creator of the website Esperfonto, describes the typeface as 'over-used', the style works particularly well when used in a religious context or as a consciously archaic form intended to evoke a sense of the past.

GOUDY TEXT

ABCDEFGHIJKLM
NOPQRSTUVWXYZ

a b c d e f g h i j k l m
n o p q r s t u v w x y z

0 1 2 3 4 5 6 7 8 9

. , & ! ? $ £ ß f @ µ ©

You must be the change you wish to see in the world

Goudy Text

Amantes sunt amentes

San Marco Roman

The past is practice

Crusader

THE PHRASES

'YOU MUST BE THE CHANGE YOU WISH TO SEE IN THE WORLD' IS A QUOTE FROM MAHATMA GANDHI, INDIAN POLITICAL AND SPIRITUAL HERO.

AMANTES SUNT AMENTES: LOVERS ARE LUNATICS (LATIN).

'THE PAST IS PRACTICE' IS A COMMON PHRASE FOR PEOPLE MOVING ON FROM STRIFE OR PAIN.

BLACKLETTER

LUCIDA BLACKLETTER

ABCDEFGHIJKLM
NOPQRSTUVWXYZ

a b c d e f g h i j k l m
n o p q r s t u v w x y z

0 1 2 3 4 5 6 7 8 9
. , & ! ? $ £ ß f @ π μ ©

Vita, si scias uti, longa est

Lucida Blackletter

Vita, si scias uti, longa est

Lucida Casual

Forever Young

Blackletter 686

THE PHRASES

Vita, si scias uti, longa est: Life is long if we know how to use it (Latin).

Tattoos have a wonderful here and now quality about them, and 'forever young' is the ultimate expression of youthful rebellion.

BLACKLETTER

american text

A B C D E F G H I J K L M
N O P Q R S T U V W X Y Z

a b c d e f g h i j k l m
n o p q r s t u v w x y z

0 1 2 3 4 5 6 7 8 9

. , & ! ? $ £ ß f @ ω µ ©

IT'S A LONG WAY TO THE TOP

American Text

It's a long way to the top

American Text

Never walk alone

Journalistic

THE PHRASES

'It's a long way to the top' is a lyric from an AC/DC song, and is a great rock and roll statement.

'Never walk alone' could be given all manner of personal meanings, but it could also evoke the song 'You'll never walk alone' originally from the musical Carousel and now popular with football club Liverpool F.C in the UK.

CASUAL SCRIPT

Casual scripts comprise all the informal scripts that are still recognisable as a form of handwriting. They form part of a diverse group of typefaces that have one characteristic in common – they all resemble some form of handwriting. They work well for a more simplistic take on the ornate formal scripts.

FINEPRINT

A B C D E F G H I J K L M
N O P Q R S T U V W X Y Z

a b c d e f g h i j k l m
n o p q r s t u v w x y z

0 1 2 3 4 5 6 7 8 9

. , & ! ? $ £ ß f @ • ©

La calma è la virtù dei forti

Fineprint Light

La calma è la virtù dei forti

Fineprint Regular

Wake My Dreams

Fineprint Swash

THE PHRASES

LA CALMA È LA VIRTÙ DEI FORTI: Calm is a virtue of the strong (Italian).

'WAKE MY DREAMS' is an increasingly popular text tattoo – its fantastical, dreamlike quality works well in small script.

CASUAL SCRIPT

PARADE

ABCDEFGHIJKLM
NOPQRSTUVWXYZ

a b c d e f g h i j k l m
n o p q r s t u v w x y z

0 1 2 3 4 5 6 7 8 9

. , & ! ? $ £ ß f

Only when the last tree has died, the last river been poisoned and the last fish been caught will we realise that we cannot eat money.

Parade

THE PHRASE

THIS NATIVE AMERICAN PROVERB IS A TIMELESS STATEMENT THAT COULD WORK WELL FOR A LARGE, STRIKING BACK TATTOO.

CASUAL SCRIPT

ADOBE FLOOD

ABCDEFGHIJKLM
NOPQRSTUVWXYZ

ABCDEFGHIJKLM
NOPQRSTUVWXYZ

0 1 2 3 4 5 6 7 8 9

., &!?$£$$ƒ@₩µ©

FAITH IS A BIRD THAT FEELS
DAWN BREAKING AND SINGS
WHILE IT IS STILL DARK

Flood

So it goes

Cascade Script Medium

alis volat propriis

Bible Script

THE PHRASES

This Scandavian saying works in Flood because it seems like a personal reminder, written by hand, for when times are hard.

Kurt Vonnegut, American novelist known for his works of satire, black comedy and science fiction, was known to say the simple three words 'So it goes' on the subject of death.

'alis volat propriis' means 'She flies with her own wings' in Latin — a popular tattoo phrase.

CASUAL SCRIPT

NANOGRAM

A B C D E F G H I J K L M

N O P Q R S T U V W X Y Z

a b c d e f g h i j k l m

n o p q r s t u v w x y z

1 2 3 4 5 6 7 8 9 0 . , &

! ? $ £ ß f @ ¬ µ ©

La vie est un combat,
lève-toi et bats-toi

Nanogram Regular

This too shall pass

Brush Script Medium

My kingdom for a kiss
upon her shoulder

Biffo MT Regular

THE PHRASES

LA VIE EST UN COMBAT, LÈVE-TOI ET BATS-TOI: LIFE IS A BATTLE, STAND UP
AND FIGHT (FRENCH).

'THIS TOO SHALL PASS' IS A BIBLICAL PHRASE FROM A STORY ABOUT KING
SOLOMON, I CORINTHIANS 10:12.

'MY KINGDOM FOR A KISS UPON HER SHOULDER' IS A LYRIC FROM JEFF
BUCKLEY'S SONG 'LOVER, YOU SHOULD HAVE COME OVER'. IT IS A POPULAR
TATTOO PHRASE FOR THE SHOULDER.

CASUAL SCRIPT

LAVENDER SCRIPT

A B C D E F G H I J K L M
N O P Q R S T U V W X Y Z

a b c d e f g h i j k l m
n o p q r s t u u w x y z

0 1 2 3 4 5 6 7 8 9

. , & ! ? $ £ B f @ ⌒ x ©

Life is a beautiful struggle

Lavender Script Regular

The journey is the reward

Pointed Brush Regular

Les vrais paradis sont les paradis qu'on a perdus

Ashley Script MT Regular

THE PHRASES

'LIFE IS A BEAUTIFUL STRUGGLE' HAS A WONDERFUL PATHOS – CELEBRATING LIFE IN ITS UGLINESS AND BEAUTY.

'THE JOURNEY IS THE REWARD' IS A TAO SAYING.

LES VRAIS PARADIS SONT LES PARADIS QU'ON A PERDUS: THE TRUE HEAVEN IS A HEAVEN THAT HAS BEEN LOST (FRENCH, MARCEL PROUST)

FORMAL SCRIPT

The design of typefaces specifically based upon the handwritten letter dates back to the very origins of type, but it has recently been revitalized by the capabilities of digital type. Few are suitable for the setting of extended passages of running text, but they all suit French, Italian or Spanish languages.

AT CITADEL SCRIPT

ABCDEFGHIJKLM
NOPQRSTUVWXYZ

a b c d e f g h i j k l m
n o p q r s t u v w x y z

0 1 2 3 4 5 6 7 8 9

. , & ! ? $ £ ß f

La vérité vaut bien qu'on passe quelques années sans la trouver

AT Citadel Script

La Vida Loca

AT Flemish Script

All that glitters is not gold

AT Sackers English Script

THE PHRASES

'La vérité vaut bien qu'on passe quelques années sans la trouver' translates from French to 'Truth is more valuable if it takes you a few years to find it'. It is attributed to the French author Pierre-Jules Renard.

La Vida Loca: The crazy life (Spanish).

'All that glitters is not gold' is known primarily from Shakespeare's *The Merchant of Venice*, Act ii, Scene VII.

FORMAL SCRIPT

AT SACKERS ENGLISH SCRIPT

A B C D E F G H I J K L M

N O P Q R S T U V W X Y Z

a b c d e f g h i j k l m

n o p q r s t u v w x y z

0 1 2 3 4 5 6 7 8 9

. , & ! ? $ £ ß f

Del male non fare e paura non avere

AT Sackers Italian Script

Be not afraid

Künstler Script Medium

Be not afraid

Künstler Script Book

Be not afraid

Künstler Script Bold

✝ THE PHRASES

DEL MALE NON FARE E PAURA NON AVERE: DO NO EVIL AND HAVE NO FEAR (ITALIAN).

'BE NOT AFRAID' COULD BE A CHILDHOOD PHRASE — HAVING IT AS A TATTOO IS A REMINDER OF COURAGE IN LATER LIFE.

FORMAL SCRIPT

AT MAHOGANY SCRIPT

ABCDEFGHIJKLM
NOPQRSTUVWXYZ

a b c d e f g h i j k l m
n o p q r s t u v w x y z

0 1 2 3 4 5 6 7 8 9

. , & ! ? $ £ ß f A

Chaos is a friend of mine

AT Mahogany Script

Vision without action is a daydream. Action without vision is a nightmare

AT Old Fashion Script

Face your truth

Nuptial Script

THE PHRASES

'CHAOS IS A FRIEND OF MINE' IS A QUOTE FROM THE SINGER AND IDOL BOB DYLAN, GIVEN IN AN INTERVIEW WITH NEWSWEEK IN 1985.

'VISION WITHOUT ACTION IS A DAYDREAM. ACTION WITHOUT VISION IS A NIGHTMARE' IS A TRANSLATION OF A JAPANESE PROVERB.

'FACE YOUR TRUTH' ADDRESSES ONE OF THE MAIN THEMES IN TATTOO SCRIPT ART – HONESTY.

FORMAL SCRIPT

AT RIVIERA SCRIPT

ABCDEFGHIJKLM
NOPQRSTUVWXYZ

a b c d e f g h i j k l m
n o p q r s t u v w x y z

0 1 2 3 4 5 6 7 8 9

. , & ! ? $ £ ß f Q

Not all those who wander are lost

AT Riviera script

Not all those who wander are lost

AT French script

Dream as if you'll live forever.
Live as if you'll die today.

Shelley Allegro script

Dream as if you'll live forever.
Live as if you'll die today

Shelley Volante script

THE PHRASES

'Not all those who wander are lost' is a quote taken from the poem 'All that is gold does not glitter' by JRR Tolkien for his fantasy novel *The Lord of the Rings – The Fellowship of the Ring*.

'Dream as if you'll love forever. Live as if you'll die today' is a quote attributed to the actor and icon James Dean.

FORMAL SCRIPT

SNELL ROUNDHAND SCRIPT

ABCDEFGHIJKLM

NOPQRSTUVWXYZ

a b c d e f g h i j k l m

n o p q r s t u v w x y z

0 1 2 3 4 5 6 7 8 9

. , & ! ? $ £ ß f @ μ ©

A bird doesn't sing because it has an answer; it sings because it has a song

Snell Roundhand Script

La belleza es tu cabeza

Snell Roundhand Bold Script

Verba volant, scripta manent

Snell Roundhand Black Script

THE PHRASES

'A BIRD DOESN'T SING..'. – THE NATURE OF THIS FONT SUITS THIS MORALISTIC AND POETIC QUOTE FROM THE AUTHOR MAYA ANGELOU.

'LA BELLEZA ES TU CABEZA' IS A POPULAR SPANISH PROVERB WHICH ROUGHLY TRANSLATES AS 'BEAUTY IS IN YOUR HEAD/IS YOUR HEAD'.

VERBA VOLANT, SCRIPTA MANENT: SPOKEN WORDS FLY AWAY, WRITTEN WORDS REMAIN (LATIN).

FORMAL SCRIPT

COPPERPLATE SCRIPT

A B C D E F G H I J K L M

N O P Q R S T U V W X Y Z

a b c d e f g h i j k l m

n o p q r s t u v w x y z

0 1 2 3 4 5 6 7 8 9

. , & ! ? $ ß ĵ

My bounty is as boundless as the sea,
My love as deep; the more I give to thee,
The more I have, for both are infinite.

Copperplate Script

Dum Spiro Spero

Ovidius Light

Dum Spiro Spero

Ovidius Demi

Dum Spiro Spero

Ovidius Bold

THE PHRASES

THIS stanza is taken from JULIET's balcony speech in WILLIAM SHAKESPEARE's play *ROMEO and JULIET*, Act ii, Scene ii.

DUM SPIRO SPERO: WHILE I breathe I hope (Latin).

DECORATED/ORNAMENTAL

Decorated or ornamental fonts have been dimensionalized, inlined, shadowed, outlined or optically distorted. They are capable of turning a simple phrase into a work of art on your body. There are whole fonts of ornaments, which work on their own or with another font, but many are exaggerated fonts which are striking for a tattoo.

ITC CARIBBEAN ROMAN

A B C D E F G H I J K L M
N O P Q R S T U V W X Y Z

A B C D E F G H I J K L M
N O P Q R S T U V W X Y Z

0 1 2 3 4 5 6 7 8 9

. , & ! ? $ £ §§ f @

DIVINITÉ LE JOUR, DÉMON LA NUIT

ITC Caribbean Roman

KNOW YOUR RIGHTS

Ironmonger Black

KNOW YOUR RIGHTS

Ironmonger Extended

THE PHRASES

THIS FRENCH MODERN-DAY PROVERB ROUGHLY TRANSLATES AS 'ANGELIC BY DAY, DEVILISH BY NIGHT'.

'KNOW YOUR RIGHTS' SUITS THIS BOLD, CAPITALIZED FONT.

DECORATED/ORNAMENTAL

BLIPPO BT BLACK

ABCDEFGHIJKLM
NOPQRSTUVWXYZ

abcdefghijklm
nopqrstuvwxyz

0 1 2 3 4 5 6 7 8 9

. , & ! ? $ £ ß ƒ @

An chuid eile dom féin

Blippo BT Black

An chuid eile dom féin

DropletLite Regular

An chuid eile dom féin

Droplet Regular

THE PHRASE

AN CHUID EILE DOM FÉIN: THE OTHER PART OF ME (GAELIC).

DECORATED/ORNAMENTAL

HAIRSPRAY REDHEAD

A B C D E F G H I J K L M
N O P Q R S T U V W X Y Z

a b c d e f g h i j k l m
n o p q r s t u v w x y z

fl fi ff ffl ffi ch ll tt p s j & &

0 1 2 3 4 5 6 7 8 9

. , & ! ? $ £ ß f ?

She flies with her own wings

Hairspray Redhead

She flies with her own wings

Hairspray Blonde

She flies with her own wings

Hairspray Brunette

fl fi ff ffl ffi ch ll tt p s j & &

Hairspray Brunette Extra

THE PHRASE

'SHE FLIES WITH HER OWN WINGS' WORKS WELL WITH THIS FONT BECAUSE OF THE WHIMSICAL, LIBERATING STYLE.

WHAT IS AN EXTRA?

AN EXTRA IN A FONT, LIKE THE BRUNETTE EXTRA ABOVE, IS AN ALTERNATIVE SET OF FONTS WITHIN THE TYPEFACE WHICH INCLUDES SYMBOLS, AMPERSANDS AND LIGATURES.

DECORATED/ORNAMENTAL

WATCH MN OUTLINE

A B C D E F G H I J K L M
N O P Q R S T U V W X Y Z

0 1 2 3 4 5 6 7 8 9

. , & ! ? $ £ ƒ ©

NEVER GIVE UP

Watch MN Outline

LIFE WON'T WAIT

Stencil BT Regular

LIFE WON'T WAIT

Stencil Regular

THE PHRASES

THESE FONTS SUIT SHORT, SNAPPY QUOTES. THEY BOTH HAVE A SIMILAR THEME — THAT OF SEIZING THE DAY AND BEING POSITIVE.

DECORATED/ORNAMENTAL

neonstream

A B C D E F G
H I J J K L M
N O P Q R S T
U V W X Y Z

a b c d e f g h i j k l m
n o p q r s t u v w x y z

0 1 2 3 4 5 6 7 8 9

. , & ! ? $ £ ß ƒ @ ƒ

what does not
kill me makes
me stronger

Neonstream

Gra Go Deo

Asphalt black Condensed

Gra Go Deo

Asphalt Black

THE PHRASES

This font has a striking neon-sign-like quality which works well with modern-day proverbs and sayings. As tattoos are often chosen during periods of change or renewal in life, phrases about becoming a stronger individual are common.

Gra Go Deo: Love forever (Gaelic).

DECORATED/ORNAMENTAL

WOODTYPE ORNAMENT ONE

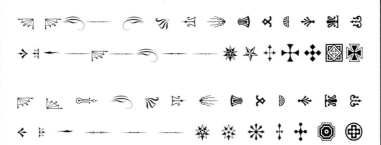

Woodtype Ornaments One

Woodtype Ornaments Two

THESE SYMBOLS COULD FRAME A PHRASE OR A WORD ON A TATTOO. THEY WOULD WORK VERY WELL GOING AROUND AN ANKLE OR THE UPPER ARM.

CALLIGRAPHIC

Calligraphic type is based on hand-rendered script letterforms. They are similar to script typefaces, but have more of a spontaneity, vitality and fluidity of form. They also have more space for variation. It is worth seeking out an unusual calligraphic font for a tattoo if you would like one with a Chinese or Japanese brushstroke font.

PRISTINA

A B C D E F G H I J K L M
N O P Q R S T U V W X Y Z

a b c d e f g h i j k l m
n o p q r s t u v w x y z

0 1 2 3 4 5 6 7 8 9
. , & ! ? $ £ ß f

Connaître son ignorance est la meilleure part de la connaissance

Pristina Plain

We need not think alike to love alike

Lucida Calligraphy Italic

We need not think alike to love alike

El Greco Regular

THE PHRASES

THIS FRENCH PROVERB ROUGHLY TRANSLATES AS 'FIGHT YOUR IGNORANCE TO REACH KNOWLEDGE'.

'WE NEED NOT THINK ALIKE TO LOVE ALIKE' IS AN ANONYMOUS PROVERB FOR THE MODERN AGE.

CALLiGRAPHiC

CALLiGRAPHiC 421

ABCDEFGHIJKLM
NOPQRSTUVWXYZ

a b c d e f g h i j k l m
n o p q r s t u v w x y z

0 1 2 3 4 5 6 7 8 9

. , & ! ? $ £ ß f @

A prayer for the wild at heart, kept in cages

Calligraphic 421 B

A prayer for the wild at heart, kept in cages

Calligraphic 810 Roman

A prayer for the wild at heart, kept in cages

Calligraphic 810 Italic

THE PHRASE

THIS QUOTE, WHICH THE AMERICAN ACTRESS ANGELINA JOLIE HAS ON HER FOREARM AS A TATTOO, IS ATTRIBUTED TO TENNESSEE WILLIAMS, AUTHOR AND PLAYWRIGHT.

CALLiGRAPHiC

CALLiGRAPHiC 810

A B C D E F G H I J K L M
N O P Q R S T U V W X Y Z

a b c d e f g h i j k l m
n o p q r s t u v w x y z

0 1 2 3 4 5 6 7 8 9

. , & ! ? $ £ ß f

Only one who has lost everything has the ability and freedom to gain everything

Calligraphica Regular

Only one who has lost everything has the ability and freedom to gain everything

Calligraphica Italic

We live by the rules of the games we play

Calligraphica Lx

We live by the rules of the games we play

Calligraphica Sx

THE PHRASES

THESE PROVERBS ARE PERFECT FOR A TATTOO – THEY ARE BOTH UPLIFTING AND CAN BE DEEPLY PERSONAL TO EACH INDIVIDUAL.

BEYOND CLASSIFICATION

Inevitably there are some fonts that resist classification because they have been designed to question typographic convention and provoke debate. Features of the fonts may have inconsistent forms and contradictory features. Although these do not work well for long portions of text, the unusual style can suit short phrases.

FAUX JAPANESE

Doubt everything. Find your own light

Faux Japanese

α β γ δ μ π ω Ω Δ ∇ Σ < ≤ ∘ ~

Ω + − = × ÷ ± ∅ ∞ #

① ② ③ ④ ⑤ ⑥ ⑦ ⑧ ⑨

⬅ ▬ ➡ ✄ ---- ✄ ⌘ ▷ ◁ △

⇧ ⇩ ⇦ ⇨ © © © ® ◁ ▷ ↑ ☎ ✆

European Pi

The Phrase

'Doubt everything, Find your own light' are believed to be the last words of Guatama Buddha in Theravada tradition.

BEYOND CLASSIFICATION

sonata

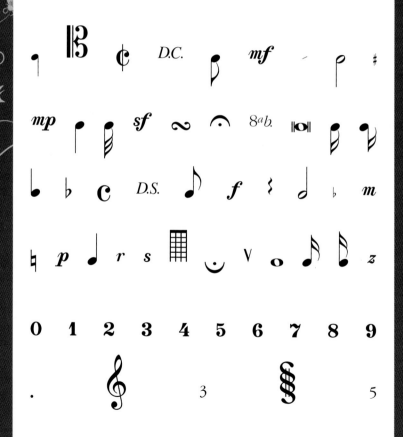

Sonata

Signs MT Regular

BEYOND CLASSIFICATION

PIXYMBOLS DECOGLASS

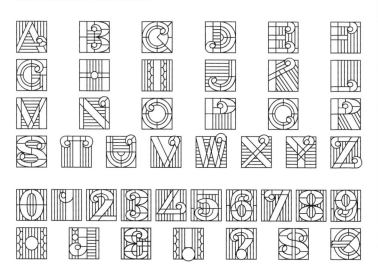

Pixymbols Decoglass

A LIFE LESS ORDINARY

ArtDeco MN Regular

THE PHRASES

This font suits simple words and is capable of speaking for itself.

'A life less ordinary' is the title of a British cult movie from 1997.

IMAGE CREDITS

All other images are the copyright of Quintet Publishing Ltd. While every effort has been made to credit contributors, Quintet Publishing would like to apologize should there have been any omissions or errors – and would be pleased to make the appropriate correction for future editions of the book.

A = above, B = below, L = left, R = right, C = centre T = top, F = far

ALAMY 59 T-L.

CORBIS 7 © Jean Leo Dugast/Sygma/Corbis; 10 © Shift Foto/Corbis; 36 T © Ulises Rodriguez/epa/Corbis; 41 © Bettmann/CORBIS; 53 T-R Corbis © Laura Levine/Corbis; 67 T-L © Jeremy Horner/CORBIS; 76 © Catherine Ivill/AMA/Corbis; 88 T-C-R © Steve Craft/Corbis; 92 T-R © Corbis Adam Blasberg; 98 T-R © Corbis; 102 T-L © Lucy Nicholson/Reuters/Corbis, T-C Corbis © KIMBERLY WHITE/Reuters/Corbis; 106 T-L © Frank Trapper/Corbis; 112 T-L © Steve Chenn/CORBIS.

DANIEL WILL-HARRIS 12.

FOTALIA 59 T-R; 61 L; 70 T-L; 80 T-L; 94 T-C.

GETTY IMAGES 3 YURI CORTEZ/AFP/Getty Images; 36 B GABRIEL BOUYS/AFP/Getty Images; 44 T-C Vince Bucci/Getty Images; 53 T-L Brian Ach/WireImage; 59 T-C Brian Ach/WireImage; 67 T-C Tony Barson/WireImage, T-R Alison Wright/National Geographic/Getty Images; 70 T-R NILS MEILVANG/AFP/Getty Images; 72 ANWAR AMRO/AFP/Getty Images; 73 Paula Bronstein/Getty Images; 74 T-R MARTIN BERNETTI/AFP/Getty Images; 77 Ethan Miller/Getty Images; 88 T-C-L Harold Cunningham/Getty Images T-R Ryan Pierse/Getty Images 94 T-R Florian Seefried/Getty Images; 98 T-L © Grant Faint/Getty Images; 102 T-R ROBYN BECK/AFP/Getty Images; 106 T-C April Brimer/Getty 108 Jamie Squire/Getty Images; 112 T-R © Arace Photographic/Getty images; 116 T-L.

INA SALTZ 15.

ISTOCK 29; 44 T-L; 53 T-C; 61 T-R; 70 T-C; 74 T-C; 88 T-L; 94 T-L; 104; 112 T-C; 114 T-R; 115 T-C, T-R.

NAGVIB & FADILLAH AT NAGFA AMBIGRAM—NAGFA.BLOGSPOT.COM 109 T-R; 110; 111 T-R.

REX FEATURES 44 T-R Stuart Atkins / Rex Features; 92 T-L CHRIS HATCHER / BEI / Rex Features; 106 T-R Jim Smeal / BEI / Rex Features.

SHUTTERSTOCK 50; 74 T-L; 80 T-C, T-R; 84 all Shutterstock; 92 T-C; 98 C; 100; 101; 103; 105 all Shutterstock; 113 all Shutterstock; 114 T-L, T-C.

W. ELDRIDGE, TATTOO ARCHIVE Photo Courtesy of Paul Rogers Tattoo Research Center: 26.

WOW TATTOOS 107; 109 T-L, B-L, B-R; 111 L. Ambigram tattoo designs by Mark Palmer, owner of WowTattoos.com and the world's leading Ambigram tattoo artist.

ACKNOWLEDGEMENTS

After writing the original *Tattoo Design Directory* in 2008, I foolishly imagined
that any subsequent volumes would issue forth with much greater ease. In the
case of this second book in the series, *Alphabets and Scripts*, nothing could be
further from the truth. All struggles aside, this volume afforded me many golden
opportunities to meet the wacky and wonderful world of characters who inhabit
the world of tattoos, typography and typefaces. Or in this case, where all three
collide in a wonderful amalgamation of alphabets and art. This book would
have been impossible without their help. I must start by thanking my researcher
and dear friend, **Robert 'PJ' Reece** as we attempted to unravel the mysteries
of typography and fonts. I could not have completed this book without PJ.
Typography is a fascinating world and one to which many have devoted their lives
and passion. I feel I barely scratched the surface, but hopefully did so in such a way
that the book serves both tattoo artists and body art enthusiasts as they explore
the universe of text tattoos. Typographically, I owe a tremendous debt of thanks to
Daniel Will–Harris and **Ina Saltz** for their insight and their interviews.
On a graphic design note, **Chris Hold**, **Shannon Hemmett** and **Dave Schmeikal**,
all avid tattoo enthusiasts in their own right, and **Johnathon Strebley** and
Alec MacNeil.

The tattoo artists and members of the tattoo community who have shared their
knowledge and stories with me are legion in number, and the following are just
some I spoke with in the past twelve months. I can start no list without mentioning
Thomas Lockhart first, as Tom is literally where it starts. Heartfelt thanks go out
to **Bob Baxter**, **Lyle Tuttle**, **C.W. 'Chuck' Eldridge**, **Harriet Cohen**,
'Shanghai' Kate Hellebrand, **Mike McCabe**, **Jack Rudy**, **Brian Everett**,
Pat Fish, **Marissa DiMattia**, **Pym Mahon**, **Lars Krutak**, **Cindy Burmeister**,
Michelle Cameron, **Vyvyn Lazonga**, **Darren Rosa**, **Henning Jörgensen**, **Peter
Feigl**, **Tony Edwards**, **Greg Piper**, **Rich Ives**, **Dana Brunson**, **Flo Makofske**, **Dave**
and **Peggy Sucher**, **Dennis Dwyer**, **Bill Hannong**, **Bill Funk**, **Dick Goldman**,
Bill DeMichele, **Jacqueline Beach**, **Greg James**, **Mr. G.**, **Sailor Bill Johnson**,
C.Byron Wallace, **Tony Olivas**, **Snake Yates**, **Lucas Hendrick** and to all others I
have inadvertently overlooked.

At my desk, my feeble grasp of modern technology was aided and abetted by a group of friends who kept my cyber lifeline connected at all times; **Patrick Gross, Justin Callison**, **Doug Cook**, **Alan Schroder** and **Wesley Gervais**. My editors at Quintet, **Asha Savjani** and **Martha Burley**, deserve special credit for putting up with me. I am grateful for their forbearance, patience, tolerance, grace and understanding during this process. Thank you to all my many friends and family, you know who you are! If I have overlooked or missed anyone, my apologies. What knowledge I have passed along comes from others far wiser than me, the mistakes are solely my own.

In deepest gratitude, **Vince Hemingson**

Quintet Publishing acknowledgements
Chinese Translation London; Erica Hatcher; Christiana Kastani; Naguib and Fadillah at Nagfa Ambigram; Asya-Miriam Platzky; Katy Sefollahi; Sheffield Typesetters; The American Sanskrit Institute.

INDEX